ENGLISH
FOR
EMPLOYMENT

BY
LARRY PARSKY, PH.D.

EDITED BY DONN MOSENFELD

PARSKY
LIFE
SKILLS
SERIES

ISBN# 0-87694-401-2   EDI 251

TABLE OF CONTENTS

REVIEW OF SENTENCE CONSTRUCTION

SENTENCE FRAGMENTS

A properly constructed sentence is a group of words that expresses a complete thought. A sentence fragment is only part of a sentence. Look over the following examples:

Fragment: Applied for a job.
(Who applied?)

Sentence: Inez applied for a job.

Fragment: While reading the Classified Section. (What happened?)

Sentence: While reading the Classified Section, Derek found an ad for the job he had just left.

Avoid sentence fragments when you write business letters or other job-related communications.

❖ Exercise 1

Directions:

Read over the examples below and identify each one as either a **Sentence** or a **Fragment**.

Fragment   1. Working on the job.

Sentence   2. Jon prepared a new résumé.

_____   3. Looking for a full-time job.

_____   4. Preparing for a job interview.

_____   5. Several students applied for the job.

_____   6. An exciting career with computers.

_____   7. There were many people in the room.

_____   8. Angela has three years of work experience.

_____   9. Mario asked important questions.

_____   10. Filling out several job applications.

_____   11. Typing a letter of application.

_____   12. I enrolled in the summer computer program.

❖ Exercise 2

Directions:

Add a word or words of your own to each sentence fragment below to make it a complete sentence. Then copy it over and add the correct punctuation at the end. If a sentence is already complete, simply add the end punctuation. Study the examples.

1. Addresses for the names of your personal references

   Where are the addresses for the names of your personal references?

2. She has the qualifications for the job

   She has the qualifications for the job.

3. Many employees were laid off

   _____

4. John's supervisor insists on workers being prompt

   _____

5. Several job applicants

   _____

6. Asking the right questions during the interview

   _____

7. Having previous job experience is important

   _____

8. Applied for the position of computer trainee

   _____

9. All applicants must have a high school diploma

   _____

10. The salary is high for an unskilled job

    _____

RUN-ON SENTENCES

A run-on sentence is two complete sentences which have been incorrectly joined together, often with no punctuation or perhaps only a comma. This type of error can easily be corrected by simply separating the sentences. Begin each of the new sentences with a capital letter. Punctuate the end of the sentence with a period, question mark, or exclamation point. Study the examples.

Run-on: Please attend a department meeting on Thursday, bring your report.

Correct: Please attend a department meeting on Thursday. Bring your report.

❖ Exercise 3

Directions:

Rewrite each run-on sentence below as two sentences. Use correct capitalization and punctuation.

1. Congratulations on your job performance you have met all your monthly goals.

   _____

   _____

2. The meeting has been canceled, it will be rescheduled.

   _____

3. I was employed as a cashier this position taught me how to manage large sums of money.

   _____

   _____

4. I can come for an interview, my telephone number is 962-3482.

   _____

   _____

5. I have completed two years in accounting and finance I have maintained an "A–" average.

   _____

   _____

❖

REVIEW OF PUNCTUATION, CAPITALIZATION, AND GRAMMAR

BASIC RULES OF CAPITALIZATION

Study the basic rules described below for capitalizing words in job-related communications and complete the accompanying exercises.

1. Capitalize each word in the greeting of a business letter.

> Dear Sir:
>
> Dear Mr. Johnson:

❖ Exercise 1

Directions:

Underline each word that should be capitalized.

> dear ms. rodriguez:
>
> dear mr. cheng:
>
> dear ms. collins:

2. Capitalize the first word in a sentence.

> Please consider me as an applicant for the job.
>
> Enclosed are the names and addresses of my references.

❖ Exercise 2

Directions:

Underline each word that should be capitalized.

I am a senior at Central High School. i am studying computer science. my grade point average is 3.5. i will graduate with honors.

3. Capitalize the first word in the closing of a business letter (but do not capitalize any other word except the first word).

Sincerely,

Yours truly, (Note that the second word, "truly," is not capitalized.)

Cordially,

❖ Exercise 3

Directions:

Underline each word that should be capitalized.

sincerely yours,

yours very truly,

fraternally yours,

4. Capitalize the names of months and days.

I have an interview on Thursday, March 4.

A meeting has been scheduled for Monday, October 4.

❖ Exercise 4

Directions:

Underline each word that should be capitalized.

We can see you on thursday, October 25.

My résumé will be typed on monday, january 16.

5. Capitalize the names of particular places and things.

City and State – I live in Atlanta, Georgia.

Street and Building – The Empire State Building is located on Fifth Avenue and West 34th Street.

Companies, Clubs, Associations, and Departments –
the **P**rudential **I**nsurance **C**ompany (Note that the "the" does not have to be capitalized unless it is a formal part of the name or the beginning of a sentence.)

Society for the **P**revention of **C**ruelty to **A**nimals

the **A**ssociation of **A**merican **R**ailroads
Accounting **D**epartment (the name of the particular department)

Schools and Universities –
L.D. Brandeis **H**igh **S**chool
the **U**niversity of **M**ichigan (Do <u>not</u> capitalize the words *of, for,* or *the* in such names.)

❖ Exercise 5

Directions:

Underline each word that should be capitalized.

1. I work at the sears towers in chicago, illinois.

2. I attend j. f. kennedy high school.

3. The bus stop is located on berg road and outer drive.

4. Did you request information from the association of american universities?

5. The globe building is located on empire boulevard.

6. She attends howard university.

7. The white house is located on pennsylvania avenue in washington, D.C.

8. The american red cross provided assistance to flood victims.

9. Ms. Rodgers is a supervisor of the billing department.

❖ Exercise 6

Directions:

Underline the letters in the sentence below that should be capitalized. Study the example.

1. <u>i</u> received information for my report from the <u>n</u>ational <u>e</u>pilepsy <u>s</u>ociety.

(continued on the next page)

2. i register for classes at union college on september 3, 199–.

3. the world trade center is located in new york, new york.

4. i am employed in the produce department of the friendly supermarket.

5. the fisher building is located on grand boulevard and second avenue.

6. she is a member of the national organization for women.

7. i have an interview in the personnel department of the national insurance company.

8. our next basketball game will be played at mumford high school.

9. i attended wayne state university in detroit, michigan.

10. did you write the american society of travel agents for career information?

11. i visited the sears tower and the field museum in chicago.

12. i met mrs. cruz on columbus avenue and west 84th street.

13. i have an appointment with mary johnson, a travel consultant.

14. i belong to the science club and the national honors society.

15. the meeting will be held on tuesday at martin luther king high school.

16. we visit my grandmother in march and august.

END PUNCTUATION

Job-related written communications should contain complete properly constructed sentences. There are four basic types of sentences: statements, questions, commands, and exclamations. Each sentence begins with a capital letter and ends with a period (.), a question mark (?), or an exclamation point (!). Study the sample sentences.

1. Consider me as an applicant for the job. *Statement*

2. Has the trainee position been filled? *Question*

3. Please be prompt. *Command*

4. Our monthly sales surpassed our estimates! *Exclamation*

❖ Exercise 7

Directions:

Put the correct punctuation mark at the end of each sentence. Then, identify the type of sentence: *Statement, Question, Command,* or *Exclamation.*

1. Send me your résumé _____

2. Do you have a job application form _____

3. I applied for the administrative assistant position _____

4. I found an excellent job _____

5. Do you have the addresses of your previous jobs _____

6. List the names and addresses of your references _____

7. The company is an Equal Opportunity Employer _____

8. Your job qualifications are superior _____

BASIC COMMA RULES

Study each of the following basic rules for using commas in job-related communications. Then complete the accompanying exercises.

1. Place a comma between the city and state or city and province or city and country.

Detroit, Michigan 48235

West Palm Beach, Florida

Toronto, Ontario

❖ Exercise 8

Directions:

Place a comma where it is needed in each example below.

He is visiting in San Antonio Texas.

I was born in Denver Colorado.

The conference will be held in Vancouver Canada.

Chicago Illinois is located on Lake Michigan.

---

2. Place a comma between the day of the month and the year.

June 8, 199_

March 31, 199_

❖ Exercise 9

Directions:

Place commas where they are needed.

School begins on September 7 199_.

My vacation starts on July 3 199_.

Your appointment is on March 24 199_.

Are you scheduled for an interview on November 15 199_?

---

3. Place a comma after the closing in a business letter.

Sincerely,

Yours truly,

❖ Exercise 10

Directions:

Place commas where they are needed.

Sincerely yours

Very truly yours

Cordially

ERRORS INVOLVING HOMONYMS

Homonyms are words that sound alike but have different meanings. A common error in writing is to use the wrong homonym in a sentence. An example is to write, "I was hear," when what you meant was, "I was here." The exercise below will help you to avoid making word usage errors of this kind.

❖ *Exercise 11*

Directions:

Each sentence below has a pair of homonyms in parentheses. Pick out the correct homonym for the sentence and copy it in the blank space. If you are unsure of an answer, check in a dictionary. Study the examples.

1. I must (**write, right**) a letter of application. *write*

2. You must find the (**write, right**) job to suit your qualifications. *right*

3. (**There, They're, Their**) is a new job posted on the bulletin board. _____

4. I mailed (**to, too, two**) job résumés. _____

5. (**There, They're, Their**) job supervisor is very strict. _____

6. Carlos has (**four, for**) years of work experience. _____

7. There were (**too, two, to**) many job applicants. _____

8. Lisa (**maid, made**) a good impression at her job interview. _____

9. A computer costs a large (**some, sum**) of money. _____

10. (**Eight, Ate**) people were interviewed for the job. _____

11. You must send (**two, to, too**) copies of your school transcript. _____

12. You must have (**sum, some**) work experience in the computer field. _____

13. (**Where, Wear**) did you mail your résumé? _____

14. Mr. Johnson interviewed (**for, four**) job applicants. _____

DOUBLE NEGATIVES

A negative word means "no." Other "no" words are *none, not, nobody, nowhere, nothing, never,* and *none.* Contractions such as *doesn't, isn't, can't, don't,* and *couldn't* are also "no" words.

Rule: **Do not use two "no" words in a sentence. Two "no" words in a sentence are referred to as a double negative.**

Example: Hector **couldn't** find **no** information. *(incorrect)*

Hector **couldn't** find **any** information. *(correct)*

Melissa **won't never** work here. *(incorrect)*

Melissa **won't ever** work here. *(correct)*

❖ Exercise 12

Directions:

Read over each sentence. Underline the word in parentheses that makes the sentence correct. Study the example.

1. José doesn't (**never,** <u>**ever**</u>) eat junk food.

2. I don't have (**no, any**) job experience.

3. Mrs. Clark doesn't go (**anywhere, nowhere**) without her watch.

4. John won't do (**anything, nothing**) after work.

5. Maria doesn't need (**any, no**) more personal references.

6. Haven't you heard (**nothing, anything**) about the new job?

7. I don't (**never, ever**) want to take a three-hour job test again!

8. Charles can't use his computer (**no more, any more**).

9. Can't you think of (**nobody, anybody**) who would like this job?

10. Sally didn't go (**nowhere, anywhere**) on her vacation.

11. He never says (**nothing, anything**) about his problems with the boss.

12. The company couldn't find (**no, any**) qualified job applicants.

❖ Exercise 13

Directions:

Each of the following sentences contains a double negative. Rewrite the sentence to make it read correctly. Study the example.

1. I haven't seen no interesting job ads.

   I haven't seen any interesting job ads.

2. Mario hasn't been to no job interviews.

   _____

3. Latanya didn't know nobody who works here.

   _____

4. Mr. Thompson doesn't never work overtime.

   _____

5. He didn't do nothing interesting on his job.

   _____

6. Mary's boss doesn't need nothing.

   _____

7. There weren't no job application forms.

   _____

8. I don't never want to work here again.

   _____

9. Her boss doesn't want to repair none of the old typewriters.

   _____

10. Carlos never works with no one.

    _____

11. Ellen didn't like none of the books.

    _____

PROOFREADING AND EDITING A MEMO

❖ Exercise 14

Directions:

Read the rough draft of a memorandum that Arlena Mendez prepared. Correct any errors in punctuation, sentence construction, and word usage by first underlining the error and writing the correction above it. Then write a final copy of the memorandum on a separate sheet of paper.

———M E M O R A N D U M———

TO: All Employees

FROM: Arlena Mendez, Supervisor

SUBJECT: Employees' Lateness to Work

DATE: May 5 199_

To many employees are reporting to work late, customers have complained that know won answers the telephone between 9:00 a.m. and 9:15 a.m. This isn't no way for employees to serve customers. If this problem continues, I will collect the time cards for any employee who has not punched in by 9:00 a.m.? company policy states that employees must report to work on time henceforth, deductions will be maid from the pay of employees who our late too work?

Your cooperation is appreciated,

Arlena Mendez

BASIC SPELLING RULES

Job-related memos and letters must be written accurately. Sentences must be well written with correct capitalization and punctuation. And words must be spelled correctly. When in doubt about the correct spelling of a word, always use the dictionary. This section reviews basic spelling rules for words that are often misspelled.

Directions:

Study each spelling rule. Then complete the exercise that follows the rule.

1. **Words containing *ei* or *ie*.**

   The rule is:

   > **Write *i* before *e***   (examples: thief, brief, yield, piece)
   >
   > **except after *c***   (examples: deceive, conceit)
   >
   > **or when sounded like "A."**   (examples: eight, weight)

❖ Exercise 1

Directions:

Spell each word correctly. Use *ie* or *ei*.

bel___f	n___ther	w___gh	rel___ve
c___ling	rev___w	n___ghbor	ch___f
n___ce	r___n	rec___pt	b___ge

2. Words ending in *y*.

When you add a suffix (examples: -ing, -er, -ness) to a word ending in *y* (example: *happy* becomes *happier*), does the *y* change to *i*? Here is the basic rule:

If the letter before the *y* is a vowel *(a, e, i, o, u)*, the *y* usually does <u>not</u> change. Example: *play* (the vowel *a* comes before the *y*) becomes *played*. *Annoy* becomes *annoying*. **Important exceptions:** pay – p*ai*d, say – s*ai*d.

But if the letter before the y is a consonant (as in hap*p*y—*p* is a consonant), **then the *y* usually changes to *i*.** Examples: *happy* becomes *happier*; *lucky* (*k* is a consonant) becomes *luckiest*.

❖ *Exercise 2*

Directions:

Spell each word correctly after adding the suffix shown.

donkey + s	_____	cry + es	_____
hurry + ed	_____	betray + ed	_____
try + es	_____	happy + ly	_____
copy + ed	_____	shady + est	_____
valley + s	_____	library + es	_____
tray + s	_____	easy + er	_____
puppy + es	_____	country + es	_____
spy + ed	_____	defy + ant	_____

3. Final silent *e*

A. Most root words ending in a silent *e* (examples: argue, share) drop the *e* when a suffix beginning with a vowel (example: *-ing*) is added.

argue + ing – arguing
(the *e* is dropped)

share + ing – sharing

move + er – mover
(the *e* in *move* is dropped)

move + able – movable

B. Most root words ending in silent *e* keep the *e* where a suffix beginning with a consonant (-ful, -ly) is added.

hope + ful – hopeful   use + ful – useful

sure + ly – surely   sincere + ly – sincerely

C. Most words that end with *-ce* and *-ge* keep the *e* when adding *-able* and *-ous*.

change + able – changeable   courage + ous – courageous

outrage + ous – outrageous   notice + able – noticeable

❖ Exercise 3

Directions:

Spell each word correctly after adding the suffix shown.

hope + less	_____	make + ing	_____
like + able	_____	fame + ous	_____
believe + ing	_____	retrace + able	_____
enforce + able	_____	take + ing	_____
arrive + al	_____	service + able	_____
care + ful	_____	bite + ing	_____
manage + able	_____	knowledge + able	_____
come + ing	_____	love + able	_____
use + age	_____	nine + ty	_____
prove + ing	_____	nice + ly	_____

4. Doubling the final consonant.

A. Consider the word *hit*. It only has one syllable. It ends in a consonant (*t*). The next to last letter is a vowel (*i*).

When you add a suffix beginning with a vowel (-*ing*, -*ed* — but not -*ful*, which begins with the consonant *f*) **to a word like *hit*** . . .

- with one syllable

- ending in a consonant

- with the next to last letter a vowel

. . . **double the last consonant.**

Examples:

hit + ing – hitting (the *t* is doubled)

beg + ed – begged

wet + est – wettest

hop + ing – hopping

But:

wet + **n**ess (-*ness* begins with the consonant *n*) becomes *wetness* (only one *t*)

ta**lk** – talked (the letter before the *k* is a consonant—do <u>not</u> double the *k*)

❖ *Exercise 4*

Directions:

Add -**ed** to each word below, doubling the root word's final consonant when you should.

1. trip + ed _____
2. skim + ed _____
3. bust + ed _____
4. hug + ed _____
5. stamp + ed _____
6. fold + ed _____
7. ban + ed _____
8. slip + ed _____

9. dip + ed _____
10. last + ed _____
11. curl + ed _____
12. wrap + ed _____
13. sand + ed _____
14. beg + ed _____
15. drop + ed _____
16. ship + ed _____

B. What about root words with *more* than one syllable?

Examples:

refer (2 syllables)

admit (2 syllables)

When you add the suffix (examples: *-ed, -ing*), pronounce the word. Does **the accent come on the last syllable** of the root word (as in *referred, admitting,* where you accent *-mit-*)? If it does, then **double the consonant.**

Examples:

forget + ing – forgetting (accent on second syllable, *-get-*)

regret + ed – regretted (accent on *-gret-*)

❖ *Exercise 5*

Directions:

Spell each word correctly by adding the suffix indicated.

sad + est	_____	confer + ed	_____
sad + ly	_____	admit + ed	_____
occur + ing	_____	swim + ing	_____
slip + ing	_____	hid + en	_____
incur + ed	_____	commit + ing	_____
begin + er	_____	skid + ed	_____
omit + ing	_____	permit + ed	_____

C. But do <u>not</u> double the consonant if the accent falls on the first syllable.

alter + ing – **al**tering (accent on *al-*, the first syllable – do <u>not</u> double the *r*)

cancel + ed – **can**celed (only one *l*)

diagram + ing – **di**agraming

benefit + ed – **ben**efited

Note the following exceptions:

kidnap + er – **kid**napper
(double *p*)

program + ed – **pro**grammed
(double *m*)

❖ *Exercise 6*

Directions:

Spell each word correctly.

profit + ed	_____	total + ing	_____
differ + ed	_____	travel + er	_____
credit + or	_____	diagram + ed	_____

---

5. The one-plus-one rule.

When the prefix (such as *dis-* or *ap-*) **of a word ends with the same letter as the first letter of the root word, be sure that both letters are included.**

dis + satisfy – dissatisfy
(double *ss*)

ap + prove – approve
(double *pp*)

mis + spell – misspell

un + necessary – unnecessary

Likewise, when the root word ends and the suffix begins with the same letter, be sure that both letters are included.

cruel + ly – cruelly (double *ll*)

usual + ly – usually

brown + ness – brownness

cool + ly – coolly

When two words are combined to make a compound word in which the last letter of the first word and the first letter of the second word are the same, the same rule applies.

book + keeper – bookkeeper

over + run – overrun

❖ Exercise 7

Directions:

Spell each word correctly.

un + noticed	_____	fatal + ly	_____
shirt + tail	_____	dis + service	_____
final + ly	_____	mis + step	_____
mean + ness	_____	hot + head	_____
re + read	_____	natural + ly	_____

❖ Exercise 8

Directions:

Read the following list of words in Column 1. If the word is spelled correctly, write **Correct** in Column 2. If the word is misspelled, spell it correctly. Study the examples.

Column 1	Column 2	Column 1	Column 2
1. sheding	*shedding*	12. copys	_____
2. taking	*Correct*	13. forgetting	_____
3. field	_____	14. nieghbor	_____
4. useage	_____	15. changeable	_____
5. skiny	_____	16. underate	_____
6. sincerely	_____	17. argueing	_____
7. credited	_____	18. hopeless	_____
8. beginning	_____	19. disimilar	_____
9. heavyset	_____	20. cruelly	_____
10. obeyed	_____	21. turkeys	_____
11. payed	_____	22. luckier	_____

❖ Exercise 9

Directions:

Spell each word correctly.

1. happy + est   _____

2. employ + able   _____

3. y___ld (*ie* or *ei*)   _____

4. hope + ful   _____

5. shop + ing   _____

6. worship + ed   _____

7. forget + ing   _____

8. employ + er   _____

9. fr___ght (*ie* or *ei*)   _____

10. ordinary + ly   _____

11. dis + similar   _____

12. safe + ty   _____

13. outrage + ous   _____

14. under + rate   _____

15. monkey + s   _____

16. admit + ing   _____

17. beauty + ful   _____

18. confer + ed   _____

19. pray + ed   _____

20. prefer + ing   _____

21. carry + ed   _____

22. n___ther (*ie* or *ei*)   _____

23. beg + ed   _____

24. sky + s   _____

25. cost + ly   _____

PROOFREADING AND EDITING A BUSINESS LETTER

❖ Exercise 10

Directions:

Read the business letter below carefully. This letter contains errors in spelling, word usage, and sentence construction. Cross out each error. Make the correction above it. Then write a final draft.

3641 Harden avenue

Atlanta GA 30324

June 3 199_

Ms. Olivia McAllister

Omni Computer company

2451 Davis Parkway

Atlanta, GA 30302

Dear Ms. McAllister:

I wood like to apply for the computer programmer trainee position that was advertised in today's Atlanta Post.

I am graduating this month from martin Luther King Community College, where I studeyed computer science, I will be graduating with honors, since i maintained a 3.9 average?

Enclosed is my résumé please telephone me at 218-5932 for an interview at your convenience. I look forward to hearing from you.

Sincerely Yours,

Ronald Johnson

Ronald Johnson

PROOFREADING AND EDITING A MEMORANDUM

❖ Exercise 11

Directions:

Read over the rough draft of a memorandum that Angela Carter prepared. Proofread and edit errors in capitalization, punctuation, and spelling. Then write a final draft.

M E M O R A N D U M

TO: All Employees

FROM: angela carter, assistant manager

SUBJECT: Vacashun Schedule

DATE: April 5, 199-

i am preparing a vacashun schedule for the time period between july 1 and December 20, pleaze send me a note indicating the two-week period that is your first choice for your vacashun. All vacashuns must begin on a monday. The week of november 20-27 is a black-out period because of the thanksgiving holiday Know more than two employees can be on vacashun during the same week?

If you do not send me your choice by April 25, i will have to schedule your vacashun for you with your cooperation I hope we will be able to work out a vacation schedule that is satisfactory to everyone.

Please see me if you have any further questions?

CORRECTION CODE

To The Student:

Some teachers use the following set of symbols to indicate the errors that have been made on written work by students. These symbols are placed in the margins opposite the errors that are to be corrected. Study the code.

¶   – Begin a new paragraph.

Cap.   – There is a capitalization error on this line.

Punct.   – There is a punctuation error in the sentence.

Sp.   – The circled word has been misspelled.

Frag.   – This is a sentence fragment (an incomplete sentence). Study the example.

         Fragment: Filled out a job application.

         Sentence: She filled out a job application.

R/O   – This is a run-on sentence. It contains two sentences punctuated as one. Study the examples:

         Run-on: Angela applied for a job she filled out a job application.

         Sentence: Angela applied for a job. She filled out a job application.

         Run-on: John completed a training program, he now works as a bank teller.

         Sentence: John completed a training program. He now works as a bank teller.

^   – A word has been left out.

?   – I do not understand what you are saying.

Wd. Usage   – You used the wrong word in the sentence

Doub. Neg.   – There are two "no" words in this sentence.

         Incorrect: Maria doesn't have no job interviews.

         Correct: Maria doesn't have any job interviews.

❖ Exercise 12

Directions:

The markings to the left of the letter below indicate what kind of corrections are to be made. Underline each error and write your correction above it. Then write a final draft on a separate sheet of paper.

Cap. 3985 Pacific avenue

Cap./Punct. los angeles ca 90082

Cap. july 15, 199_

Cap. Tracy's department store

Ms. Hillary Walters

Cap. 1436 Fairfax boulevard

Cap./Punct. los angeles ca 90025

Cap./Wd. Usage deer Ms. Walters:

Sp. I have been emploied in the Housewars Department for two

R/O/Sp. years I have a good attendance record. I have also recieved

Punct. satisfactory work evaluations

Sp./Cap. An emergence has occured in my family, and i must request

Sp./R/O/Cap. permision to deal with the crisis my six-year-old daughter just

∧ had surgery. No one at home when she is released from the

Cap./Sp. hospital. Therefore, i am requesting a two-weak leave of ab-

Cap./Punct. sence between july 22 and august 4

R/O I appreciate your understanding I hope that you will ap-

Punct. prove my request

Sp./Cap. Sincerly Yours,

Viola Mitchell

Viola Mitchell

DEVELOPING AN EMPLOYMENT VOCABULARY

The 40 words in this chapter are used over and over again in the world of work. Learning them will help you—

- fill out job application forms
- prepare a résumé

- fill out applications for credit, Social Security, etc.
- understand better the questions you are asked on job interviews
- fill out employment forms for your employer

❖ Exercise One

Directions:

The following words are words you encounter when you hunt for a job.

WORDS TO KNOW		
applicant	job interview	résumé
position desired	salary desired	

Read each sentence carefully and figure out the meaning of the **bold-face** word. If you are unsure, use a dictionary to find the correct meaning.

1. The Public Utility Company received more than 50 telephone calls from **applicants** interested in the job it advertised in yesterday's *Journal Times*.

   An **applicant** is

   a. a form the employer asks job seekers to fill out

   b. an employer who has a job opening

   c. a job seeker

2. The applicant wore a new suit to the **job interview** and came prepared to answer any questions the interviewer might have.

   A job interview is a meeting between

   a. a job applicant and an employer

   b. a worker on the job and a boss

   c. two workers discussing how to do something

3. Your **résumé** should be typed. It should list all the schools you attended and all the jobs you have had.

   A résumé is

   a. a permission slip

   b. a successful job interview

   c. a written summary of a job applicant's experiences and skills

4. The employer may have more than one available job. That is why application forms sometimes ask you to list the **position desired.**

   A position desired is

   a. a job you had

   b. a job you want

   c. your goal in life

5. The applicant listed the minimum wage for **salary desired** since she had no previous work experience.

   The **salary desired** is

   a. a salary that is much better than the applicant expects to receive

   b. a salary the applicant feels is acceptable for the job

   c. an unacceptable salary

❖ Exercise Two

Directions:

Below are five more words you need to know when you are looking for a job. These words all occur frequently on job application forms.

WORDS TO KNOW		
present address	previous address	spouse
marital status	maiden name	

1. Maria has been living at her **present address** for three years. Before that she lived with her parents.

   Your **present address** is

   a. where you used to live

   b. where you live now

   c. where you plan to live

2. John could not remember his **previous address**.

   Your **previous address** is

   a. where you used to live

   b. where you live now

   c. where you plan to live

3. Alfred is not married; he doesn't have a **spouse**.

   A **spouse** is

   a. a brother or sister

   b. a husband or wife

   c. a mother or father

4. If you have never been married, check the box that says "single" where the form asks you your **marital status.**

Your **marital status** is

a. what you think about marriage

b. what your marriage is like

c. whether you are married or divorced or widowed, etc.

5. Jenny's father is Howard Smith. Her husband is Carl Hankins. So her married name is Jenny Hankins. Her **maiden name** is Jenny Smith.

A **maiden name** is

a. a woman's first name

b. a woman's full married name

c. a woman's name before she got married

❖ Exercise Three

Directions:

Decide which word or phrase makes the best sense in each of the following sentences.

WORDS TO KNOW		
applicant	marital status	position desired
résumé	spouse	

1. You used to be married, but is that still your _____

_____ ?

2. Mary was the only female _____ who was able to get a job interview.

3. The company did not have a job opening for the _____

_____ that Chung Li listed.

4. Albert sent the company his _____
when he applied for the job.

5. Helen Roberts' _____ is John Roberts; they've been married for seven years.

❖ Exercise Four

Directions:

Decide which word or phrase makes the best sense in each of the following sentences.

WORDS TO KNOW		
job interview	maiden name	present address
previous address	salary desired	

1. One of the toughest questions to answer in a _____

_____ is why you left your last job.

2. List a realistic figure when you are asked the _____

_____ .

3. Some people have always lived at the same address; they have no

_____ .

4. Your _____ is where you get your mail.

5. A woman can keep her _____ after she gets married if she wants to.

❖ Exercise Five

Directions:

Read each sentence carefully and figure out the meaning of the **bold-face** word. If you are unsure, use a dictionary to find the correct meaning.

WORDS TO KNOW

employee	occupation	supervisor
probation	Equal Opportunity Employer	

1. Melinda is an **employee** of the Harris Company. She works in their warehouse.

   An **employee** is

   a. a boss

   b. a friend

   c. a worker

2. Karen is a bookkeeper. Andrea is the office manager. Steve is a sales coordinator. What is your **occupation**?

   Your **occupation** is

   a. the location of the company you work for

   b. the title or type of job you have

   c. the type of business your employer is in

3. Joe reports to his **supervisor** whenever he has a problem on the job.

   A **supervisor** is

   a. a boss

   b. a friend

   c. a worker

4. New employees in the Harris Company are placed on **probation** for three months. This gives the company a chance to check on their work to see if it wants to keep them on as regular members of its work force.

   Probation, as used here, means

   a. a crime committed by an employee

   b. a report on an employee's work habits

   c. a trial period for a new worker

5. **Equal Opportunity Employers** agree to hire new workers and promote people within the company without regard to such things as race, sex, creed, or ethnic origin.

   By being an **Equal Opportunity Employer**, a company helps protect the rights of

   a. workers

   b. other employers

   c. customers

❖ Exercise Six

Directions:

Read each sentence carefully and figure out the meaning of the **bold-face** word. If you are unsure, use a dictionary to find the correct meaning.

WORDS TO KNOW		
creed	ethnic origin	dependents
emergency	Social Security	

1. Catholics, Jews, and all people, no matter what their **creed**, have equal chances of being hired by an Equal Opportunity Employer.

   The word **creed** refers to

   a. a person's set of religious beliefs

   b. the color of the person's skin

   c. whether the person is male or female

2. Mrs. Liu was afraid she would be turned down for the job because she is Chinese. But it is against the law to deny a person a job on the basis of his or her **ethnic origin**.

   Ethnic origin is a way of classifying people in terms of

   a. their beliefs

   b. their education and job skills

   c. their culture, language, and customs

3. Ramon is a **dependent** of his parents. But when he graduates from high school, he plans to get a job and support himself.

   A **dependent** is a person who

   a. is supported by another person

   b. supports another person

   c. works for another person

4. An employer has to know what relative or other person to contact in case a worker gets involved in an accident on the job or has some other kind of **emergency**.

   An **emergency** is

   a. an important on-the-job event

   b. a serious or unexpected problem

   c. money owed a relative

5. Whenever you draw a salary, part of your pay is taken out and paid in to **Social Security**. Then when you retire, Social Security gives you money to live on.

   Social Security is

   a. a U.S. Government information service

   b. a U.S. Government police force

   c. a U.S. Government retirement fund

❖ Exercise Seven

Directions:

Decide which word or phrase makes the best sense in each of the following sentences.

WORDS TO KNOW		
Equal Opportunity Employer		emergency
probation	ethnic origins	dependents

1. The United States population includes people with all kinds of differ
   ent _____ .

2. Mrs. Colon supports four _____ .

3. An employee who has just been hired and is on _____
   _____ is carefully observed by a supervisor.

4. A worker's employer usually wants to know the telephone number of a
   person to contact in case of _____ .

5. Before the company became a(n) _____ ,
   it hardly ever hired women.

❖ Exercise Eight

WORDS TO KNOW		
employee	occupation	supervisor
Social Security	creed	

1. The words worker and _____ have similar meanings.

2. The words boss and _____ have similar meanings.

3. Computer programming is a good _____ .

4. Everyone who works has to have a(n) _____
   number.

5. Your beliefs about the hereafter are part of your _____ .

❖ Exercise Nine

Directions:

Try to figure out the meaning of the **bold-face** word from its use in the sentence. If you are unsure, use a dictionary.

WORDS TO KNOW		
present employer	previous employer	reference
relationship	extracurricular activities	

1. Kim informed her **present employer** that she was looking for another job.

   Your **present employer** is

   a. where you used to work

   b. where you work now

   c. where you would like to work

2. George's **previous employer** could not find a qualified person to replace him.

   Your **previous employer** is

   a. where you used to work

   b. where you work now

   c. where you would like to work

3. The application form asked Betty to list three **references**. She listed her minister and two of her teachers who she was sure would recommend her for the job.

   A **reference**, as used here, means

   a. a book in the library

   b. a description of something that happened in the past

   c. a responsible person who can describe your character

4. The form asked each employee to list the person to notify in case of an emergency. It also asked the **relationship** of that person to the employee (that is, mother, father, aunt, uncle, friend, etc.)

   A used here, **relationship** refers to

   a. family ties

   b. job history

   c. education

5. The school football team and the school debating team are examples of **extracurricular activities**.

   Extracurricular activities are

   a. the honors you received in school

   b. school activities that take place after school

   c. your favorite school subjects

❖ *Exercise Ten*

Directions:

Again, try to figure out the meaning of the word from the way it is used.

WORDS TO KNOW		
misdemeanor	felony	laid off
discharged	bonded	

1. A traffic violation is considered a **misdemeanor**.

   A **misdemeanor** is

   a. a minor crime

   b. a serious crime

   c. an unproven crime

2. Robbery and murder are **felonies**.

   A **felony** is

   a. a minor crime

   b. an unproven crime

   c. a serious crime

3. The company **laid off** many workers to save money when it started having trouble with the bank.

   A worker who has been **laid off**

   a. got sick and cannot find a job

   b. lost his or her job when the company cut back its costs

   c. quit and found a new job

4. She was **discharged** from her job because of a poor attendance record.

   To be **discharged** means to be

   a. allowed to leave

   b. fired

   c. promoted

5. People whose jobs require them to handle money are sometimes **bonded**. Companies require this to make sure they are protected in case the employee steals.

   As used here, a person who is **bonded** is

   a. insured as regards theft of company money

   b. tied to the company

   c. unable to cash checks

❖ Exercise Eleven

Directions:

Decide which word or phrase makes the best sense in each of the following sentences.

WORDS TO KNOW		
bonded	laid off	reference
relationship	extracurricular activities	

1. It is unlikely that a person with a police record can be _____ _____ .

2. Even if you have performed well on your job, you still could be _____ if your employer feels it has to reduce its costs.

3. Before you list someone as a(n) _____ , ask permission.

4. His after-school job made it difficult for Hector to participate in _____ .

5. The insurance company needs to know whom to notify in case of death and the _____ of that person to the person who is insured.

❖ Exercise Twelve

WORDS TO KNOW		
discharge	felony	misdemeanor
present employer	previous employer	

1. Jane now works at Delta Airlines. Her _____ was United Airlines.

2. Alex's _____ expects him to work on Sundays.

3. A person who has committed a _____ may have trouble getting a job.

4. The company has the right to _____ workers who do not follow the safety rules.

5. In our town it is a _____ to throw trash on the street.

❖ Exercise Thirteen

Directions:

The following words are often found in statements appearing at the end of job application forms.

Try to figure out the meaning of these words from the way they are used below.

WORDS TO KNOW		
abide by	authorize	dismissal
falsify	inquire	

1. If you sign a contract, you must **abide by** the terms of the agreement.

   To **abide by** means
   a. to change as necessary
   b. to act according to
   c. to understand

2. If you **authorize** the company to contact your references, they have every right to do so.

   To **authorize** means
   a. to give permission
   b. to give orders
   c. to refuse

3. If you include false information on a job application, you risk **dismissal** from your job.

   Dismissal means
   a. being an unhappy worker
   b. getting along well with other workers
   c. getting fired

4. It is better to tell the truth than to **falsify** information on a job application.

   To **falsify** means

   a. to give incorrect information

   b. to include all the important facts

   c. to present information in a confusing way

5. Employers who are considering a job applicant often **inquire** from previous employers about what kind of worker the applicant was.

   To **inquire** means

   a. hold back information

   b. demand payment

   c. ask questions

❖ Exercise Fourteen

Directions:

Below are five more words that are often found in the statements that appear at the end of job application forms.

WORDS TO KNOW		
investigate	terminate	omission
qualifications	misrepresentation	

1. One way to **investigate** the truth about information on a job application is to contact the applicant's previous employers.

   To **investigate** means

   a. to read

   b. to hide

   c. to check on

2. It is a **misrepresentation** of fact to say you graduated from high school when you actually dropped out in the tenth grade.

   Misrepresentation is

   a. giving false information

   b. repeating something

   c. speaking clearly

3. You should make sure you answer all the questions on the form. Before you hand it in, check for **omissions**.

   An **omission** is

   a. a difficult question

   b. a spelling error

   c. information that has been left out

4. Among the **qualifications** required for a job as a secretary are typing and shorthand.

   Qualifications are

   a. necessary requirements

   b. people considered for a job

   c. wishes

5. He is looking for a job. His previous employer **terminated** him when he got in a fist fight with his supervisor.

   To be **terminated** means

   a. to lose an argument

   b. to get fired

   c. to move around

❖ Exercise Fifteen

Directions:

Decide which word makes the best sense in each of the following sentences.

WORDS TO KNOW		
abide by	authorize	falsify
inquire	terminate	

1. To **dismiss** a person from a job means the same as to _____ _____ the person.

2. To **misrepresent** information on an application form means the same as to _____ .

3. To **investigate** means the same as to _____ .

4. If you haven't told your present employer you are looking for a job, you may not want to _____ the interviewer to call your boss.

5. She agreed to _____ the rules but then paid no attention to them.

❖ Exercise Sixteen

Directions:

Match the words in Column 1 with the definitions or examples in Column 2.

	Column 1	Column 2
_____	1. position desired	A. a person who you think will speak highly of you
_____	2. spouse	B. the person you are married to
_____	3. omission	C. the job you want
_____	4. qualification	D. a question you forgot to answer
_____	5. reference	E. a skill needed for the job

❖ Exercise Seventeen

	Column 1	Column 2
_____	1. probation	A. a mother's baby daughter
_____	2. résumé	B. engineer
_____	3. occupation	C. job hunter
_____	4. dependent	D. trial period
_____	5. applicant	E. a neat summary of your background

❖ Exercise Eighteen

	Column 1	Column 2
_____	1. previous	A. out of work
_____	2. present	B. allow
_____	3. bonded	C. insured against theft
_____	4. laid off	D. now
_____	5. authorize	E. before

❖ Exercise Nineteen

	Column 1	Column 2
_____	1. creed	A. burning down a building
_____	2. felony	B. making too much noise
_____	3. ethnic origin	C. believing in God
_____	4. misdemeanor	D. being Mexican
_____	5. extracurricular activity	E. playing in the band

❖ Exercise Twenty

	Column 1	Column 2
_____	1. marital status	A. lie
_____	2. maiden name	B. what a woman's parents called her
_____	3. Social Security	C. divorced
_____	4. misrepresentation	D. heart attack
_____	5. emergency	E. where part of your salary goes

WRITING BUSINESS LETTERS

Have you formulated career goals? Can you find career information that will help you make important career decisions? Once you have a career goal, do you know how to prepare for a job? You may be surprised to know that basic writing skills are important in preparing for a career and maintaining a job. Writing business letters is one of the most important of these skills. It is also a skill you will require throughout your adult life.

In this unit you will learn how to write six types of business letters. The first focus is on career preparation: requesting career information, and applying for a job. The second focus is on letters you write on the job: ordering merchandise, letters of complaint, letters requesting permission.

GENERAL APPROACH TO BUSINESS LETTERS

The following suggestions will help you write a business letter correctly:

1. Use correct business letter form. Study the style sheet on page 49. It summarizes the correct form for business letters along with basic letter writing rules. You may also refer to the sample business letter on page 47.

2. Type it, if possible. Otherwise be sure that your handwriting is legible. Do not print.

3. Use 8-1/2 by 11-inch unlined paper. If the letter is to be handwritten, place an 8-1/2 x 11-inch sheet of lined paper under the unlined paper. The lines from the lined paper will guide you in writing evenly and neatly on the unlined paper.

4. Make sure that your letter is brief, concise, and easy to understand.

5. Get to the point immediately. In most letters, you will want to state your reason for writing in the first or second sentence. Then provide essential background details, as needed. Do not give unessential information.

6. Proofread and edit your first draft. Use the correction code on page 26 to help you identify any writing errors. Then write your final draft.

SAMPLE BUSINESS LETTER: REQUESTING CAREER INFORMATION

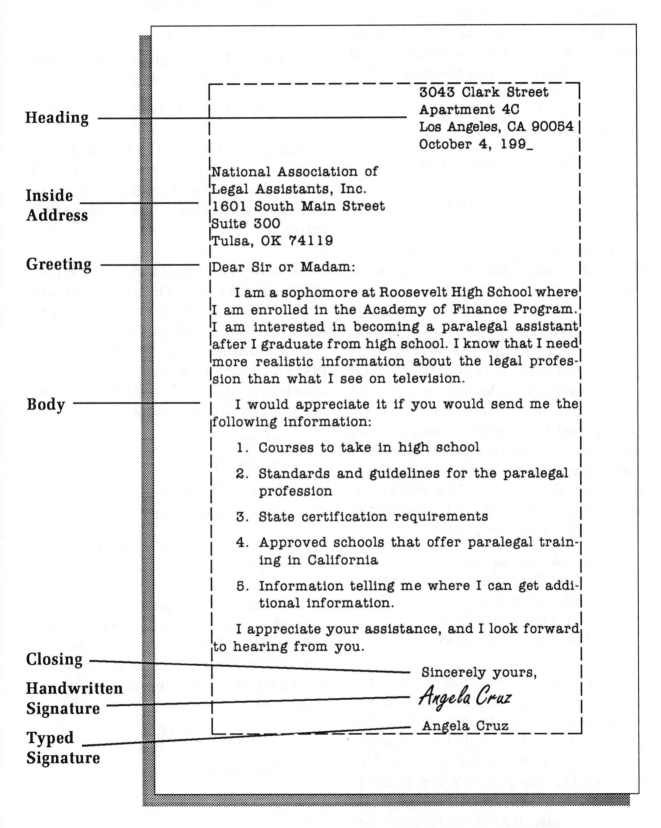

Heading

3043 Clark Street
Apartment 4C
Los Angeles, CA 90054
October 4, 199_

Inside Address

National Association of
Legal Assistants, Inc.
1601 South Main Street
Suite 300
Tulsa, OK 74119

Greeting

Dear Sir or Madam:

Body

I am a sophomore at Roosevelt High School where I am enrolled in the Academy of Finance Program. I am interested in becoming a paralegal assistant after I graduate from high school. I know that I need more realistic information about the legal profession than what I see on television.

I would appreciate it if you would send me the following information:

1. Courses to take in high school

2. Standards and guidelines for the paralegal profession

3. State certification requirements

4. Approved schools that offer paralegal training in California

5. Information telling me where I can get additional information.

I appreciate your assistance, and I look forward to hearing from you.

Closing

Sincerely yours,

Handwritten Signature

Angela Cruz

Typed Signature

Angela Cruz

Use 1-inch margins on all four sides of letter.

A business letter should contain the following parts:

Heading. The heading is the first part of a business letter. As in a friendly letter, it should include three to five lines for the address of the sender (include zip code) and date. The heading is placed in the top right corner of the letter.

2054 Mark Twain Avenue
Apartment 3A
St. Louis, MO 63105
May 4, 199_

As you know, you can abbreviate the name of a state. See the list of state abbreviations on page 128.

Inside address. The inside address is the second part of a business letter. It usually includes the name of the person you are writing to, his or her title and department, the name of the company, and the mailing address. In some cases, the name and address of the company are sufficient, without the person's name, title, and department. The inside address is placed on the left side of the letter, just above the greeting.

Mr. Donald Lewis,
   Vice President – Personnel
Media Graphics, Inc.
2046 Madison Avenue
New York, NY 10015

Greeting. The greeting is the next part of a business letter. It is contained on one line and has three parts. The first part is usually the word *Dear.* The second part includes a title, such as *Mr., Mrs.,* or *Dr.* The person's last name is the final part. In a business letter, a colon (:) is placed after the person's last name instead of a comma.

Here are examples:

Dear Mr. Lerma:

Dear Ms. Williams:

Dear Dr. Chung:

Use the following greeting when you do not have an individual's name:

Dear Sir or Madam:

Body. The body is the fourth part of a business letter. It is the main part. It should be brief and contain an introduction, a summary, and a requested action.

Closing. The closing is the fifth part of a business letter. This tells the reader that you are ending the letter. Capitalize the first word in the closing. Do not capitalize any of the other words. Place a comma (,) at the end. In a business letter, you should use a formal closing such as the following:

Sincerely,

Yours truly,

Sincerely yours,

Very truly yours,

Do not use such closings as *Fondly* or *Your friend.*

Signature. The signature is the last part of a business letter. The sender writes his or her full name at the bottom of the letter. If the letter is typed, the signature is written just above the typed name.

Rosemarie Malloy

Rosemarie Malloy

STYLE SHEET FOR A BUSINESS LETTER

Directions:

Study the outline below to strengthen your knowledge of the organization of a business letter.

Except for the state abbreviations, use no abbreviations.

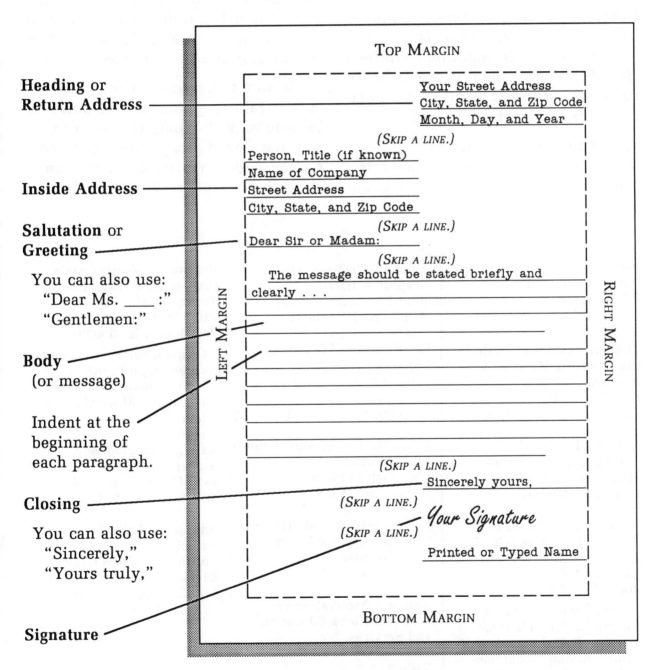

Heading or **Return Address**
- Your Street Address
- City, State, and Zip Code
- Month, Day, and Year

(SKIP A LINE.)

Inside Address
- Person, Title (if known)
- Name of Company
- Street Address
- City, State, and Zip Code

(SKIP A LINE.)

Salutation or **Greeting**
- Dear Sir or Madam:

You can also use:
"Dear Ms. ___:"
"Gentlemen:"

(SKIP A LINE.)

Body (or message)
- The message should be stated briefly and clearly . . .

Indent at the beginning of each paragraph.

(SKIP A LINE.)

Closing
- Sincerely yours,

You can also use:
"Sincerely,"
"Yours truly,"

(SKIP A LINE.)

Signature
- Your Signature

(SKIP A LINE.)

Printed or Typed Name

TOP MARGIN

LEFT MARGIN

RIGHT MARGIN

BOTTOM MARGIN

Each side should have 1-inch margins.

❖ Exercise One

Write a letter requesting career information.

Directions:

From the list below, choose an organization that relates to your present career goals. Or if you don't find an appropriate listing there, go to the library to obtain one. The series titled **Career Information Center,** published by Glencoe Publishing Co., is an excellent source. **The Occupational Outlook Handbook,** published by the U.S. Department of Labor, Bureau of Labor Statistics, is another useful source.

Then write a letter requesting information about the occupation that interests you. Request information about education and training requirements. If you are a high school student, find out which courses you should take before you graduate. Ask for a list of approved schools or training programs in your state that offer training. You might also want to request information about state certification and licensing requirements.

Be sure to use correct punctuation, capitalization, grammar, and business letter form. Write complete sentences in well-developed paragraphs. Use the correction code on page 26 to proofread and edit your letter. Write a final draft.

American Association for
Paralegal Education
P.O. Box 40244
Overland Park, KS 66204

The Educational Institute of
the American Hotel & Motel
Association
P.O. Box 1240
East Lansing, MI 48826

National Electrical
Contractors Association
7315 Wisconsin Avenue
Bethesda, MD 20814

National Association of
Trade & Technical Schools
Department BL
P.O. Box 10429
Rockville, MD 20849

(Send for a directory of accredited private trade and technical schools that offer training in automotive body repair, culinary arts, and welding.)

American Institute of
Graphic Artists
1059 Third Avenue
New York, NY 10021

Certification of Computer
Professionals
2200 East Devon Avenue
Suite 268
Des Plaines, IL 60018

Photo Marketing Association
International
3000 Picture Place
Jackson, MI 49201

Floor Covering Installation
Contractors Association
P.O. Box 2048
Dalton, GA 30722

National Association for
Practical Nurse Education
and Services, Inc.
1400 Spring Street
Suite 310
Silver Springs, MD 20910

Registered Medical Assistants of American Medical
Technologists
710 Higgins Road
Park Ridge, IL 60068

(Request information about career opportunities and requirements for taking the Registered Medical Assistant Certificate exam.)

National Cosmetology
Association, Inc.
3510 Olive Street
St. Louis, MO 63103

American Medical
Association
Division of Allied Health
Education and Accreditation
535 N. Dearborn Street
Chicago, IL 60610

(list continues on the next page)

The National Association
for Homecare
519 C Street NE
Washington, D.C. 20062

(Information for home-makers—home health aides.)

Dental Assisting National
Board, Inc.
216 E. Ontario Street
Chicago, IL 60611

Education Council of the
Graphic Arts Industry
4615 Forbes Avenue
Pittsburgh, PA 15213

(Information on schools that offer courses in printing technology.)

National Automotive
Technician Education
Foundation
13505 Dulles Technology Dr.
Herndon, VA 22071-3415

Foundation for Interior
Design Educational Research
60 Monroe Center NW
Grand Rapids, MI 49503

Association of Independent
Colleges and Schools
1 Dupont Circle NW
Suite 350
Washington, D.C. 20003

(Send for brochures describing careers as a bookkeeper, accountant, shorthand reporter, and court reporter.)

Information on Automotive Sponsored 2-Year Associate Degree Programs in Automotive Service Technology

ASSET Program Training
Department
Ford Parts and Service
Division
Ford Motor Company
Dearborn, MI 48121

Chrysler Dealer
Apprenticeship Program
National C.A.P. Coordinator
26001 Lawrence Avenue
Centerline, MI 48015

General Motors Service
Education Program
National College Coordinator
General Motors Technical
Service
30501 Van Dyke Avenue
Warren, MI 48090

Society of American Florists
1601 Duke Street
Alexandria, VA 22314

The Institute of Certified
Travel Agents
148 Linden Street
P.O. Box 56
Wellesley, MA 02181

Professional Truck Driver
Institute of America
8788 Elk Grove Boulevard
Suite M
Elk Grove, CA 95624

Council on Hotel,
Restaurant and
Institutional Education
1200 17th Street NW
Washington, D.C.
20036-3097

PROOFREADING AND EDITING A BUSINESS LETTER

The writer of a business letter should make sure to use correct business letter form, and should proofread and edit the letter carefully to make sure it has grammatically correct sentences, correct spelling, and correct capitalization and punctuation.

❖ *Exercise Two*

Directions:

Read the business letters on pages 52 and 53 carefully. One is well written, the other poorly written. When you have studied both, use the correction code sheet on page 26 to proofread and edit the poorly written letter.

1. Mark the correction code symbol for each error. Put the symbol in the left margin.

2. Cross out each error and write the correction above it.

3. Check the style sheet on page 49 to make sure the form of the letter is correct.

4. If you disagree with how a part of the letter was written, change it.

5. When you have corrected all errors and rewritten the badly written part, copy the letter on a separate sheet of paper.

3064 Glendale Avenue
Apartment 302
Tucson, AZ 85275
September 4, 19__

Mr. Roger Clark, Personnel Manager
Marshall Department Store
2046 Main Street
Tucson, AZ 85283

Dear Mr. Clark:

I appreciate having been one of the final applicants to be interviewed for the salesperson position in the new Sport's World Department. If I am hired, my enthusiasm for athletics and my knack for helping people will contribute to the department's success. Again, I hope that I presented my creative ideas for possible promotions during the interview.

I realize that all the applicants for the position have outstanding qualifications. Even if I am not selected, it was a privlege to have been considered among the best candidates for the position.

Once more, thank you for considering me for the position.

Sincerely yours,

Jason Guzman

Jason Guzman

2019 Vassar boulevard

Apartment 4B

Tucson AZ 85289

September 4, 19__

Mr. Roger Clark, Personnel Director

Marshall Department Store

2046 main street

Tucson, AZ 85283

Dear Mr. Clark,

thank you for interviewing me yesterday for the position.
I like the new idea for the department. I know that I will be
able two do the job well if I am hired everyone tells me how
good I am.

I hop that i convinced you how much I need the job, you
won't never be sorry if you hired me. I promise that I will be
the best employee your store has ever had?

Again, please consider me for the job. look forward to
hearing from you

Sincerly Yours

Kenneth Baxter

Kenneth Baxter

BUSINESS LETTERS YOU WRITE ON THE JOB

There are many situations on the job requiring you to write business letters. For instance, you work overtime and do not receive the pay on your paycheck. You need to request permission to take time off from work. Your supervisor asks you to order merchandise for your department. All these situations may require you to write business letters. These are only a few examples. In the next few lessons, you will apply basic letter-writing skills to:

1. order merchandise

2. state a complaint

3. request permission for something

ORDERING MERCHANDISE BY MAIL

Businesses often order merchandise by mail. Since such orders often involve large sums of money, these orders must be stated in writing. Ordering merchandise is often done by means of a letter. A written order accomplishes several things. It is precise—it lets both parties know what is expected. It is also a written record of what was purchased so that if there is a problem the letter can be referred to.

A letter ordering merchandise should include:

1. **Information about the sender.**

   - *Who* should receive the order:

     Gino Minetti, Manager

   - *Where* the order should be mailed:

     Pizza Passion
     4863 Lemoine Avenue
     Nashville, TN 37212

   - *When* the order was placed:

     May 3, 19__

2. **Information about the merchandise.**

   - Exactly *what* items are being ordered:

     T-Shirts

   - *How many* (quantity) are being ordered?:

     10 T-Shirts

     12 T-Shirts

     8 T-Shirts

   - *Details* about the merchandise (color, catalog number, size, dimensions) being ordered:

     10 T-Shirts (Catalog No. 3068)
     Size Large

     12 T-Shirts (Catalog No. 3067)
     Size Medium

     8 T-Shirts (Catalog No. 3066)
     Size Small

3. Method of payment and total price.

Figure out the subtotal for each item.

10 T-Shirts (Catalog No. 3068)	– Size Large	@ $5.95		$59.50
12 T-Shirts (Catalog No. 3067)	– Size Medium	@ $5.95		71.40
8 T-Shirts (Catalog No. 3066)	– Size Small	@ $5.95	+	47.60
		Sub Total		$178.50
		Shipping & handling	+	12.75
		Total Price of Order:		$191.25

- **Method of Payment:** check, money order, cashier's check, credit card, or C.O.D. (cash on delivery). If you pay by money order or cashier's check, be sure to keep a copy in case it is lost.

FAXING BUSINESS CORRESPONDENCE

Until recently, business correspondence could only be sent through the mail. Now there is a quicker way—using a *fax machine.*

A fax (which is a short term for a *facsimile*, or copy) machine is a photocopying machine connected to a telephone. It makes it possible to transmit documents over any distance almost as fast as you can place a telephone call. You can even send a copy of a picture.

A fax machine has its own telephone number. The document is placed in the fax machine and the phone number of the receiving fax machine is dialed. When the connection has been made, a copy of the document is "sent" over the telephone line, where it appears out of the receiving fax machine. The sending machine then informs you that your document has or has not been received.

Fax machines are used every day by businesses for sending letters and documents and placing orders with suppliers. Job applicants can also use faxing in some situations to send their letters and résumés to follow up on job leads.

What can job applicants do if they do not have a fax machine? Simple. They can take their résumés and letters to a photocopy center which offers fax services. There is a small charge for each page that is faxed. In seconds, a letter and résumé is in the hands of the potential employer.

4863 Lemoine Avenue
Nashville, TN 37212
May 3, 19__

T-Shirts Unlimited
1245 Fifth Avenue
Department DM
New York, NY 10003

Dear Sir or Madam:

My customers have requested that I sell T-Shirts for my pizzeria, Pizza Passion. Therefore, I would like to order a limited number of T-Shirts with the inscription "Pizza Passion" on a pizza logo.

Please send me the following:

10 T-Shirts (Catalog No. 3068)		
Size Large @ $5.95		$59.50
12 T-Shirts (Catalog No. 3067)		
Size Medium @ $5.95		71.40
8 T-Shirts (Catalog No. 3066)		
Size Small @ $5.95		+ 47.60
	Sub Total	$178.50
	Shipping & Handling	+ 12.75
	Total Price	$191.25

Enclosed is a check for $191.25 as full payment for my order.

I appreciate your prompt attention.

Sincerely,

Gino Minetti

Gino Minetti
Manager

❖ Exercise Three

Directions:

You are manager of Cookies Galore, which is located in the Northland Mall. Write a business letter to Star Promotions, Inc., 2432 Hudson Street, Your City, State, and Zip Code, to order the following holiday items:

- 8 dozen ballpoint pens with the inscription "Happy Holidays from Cookies Galore."

    (Catalog No. A-2145)
    @ $5.99 per dozen

- 3 dozen calendars for the new year with the inscription "Best Wishes for the New Year, Cookies Galore."

    (Catalog No. C-88521)
    @ $9.60 per dozen

- 4 boxes of Holiday Greeting Cards

    (Catalog No. D-5896)
    @ $7.95 per dozen

Since you receive your business mail at home, use your own address for the inside address.

1. Use acceptable business letter form. Refer to the style sheet on page 49.

2. Use correct capitalization and punctuation.

3. Write complete sentences in well-developed paragraphs. Give complete information. In your letter:

    A. List all the items, one below the other, each with its price and catalog number.

    B. Figure out the subtotal.

    C. For sales tax, use the sales tax rate for your state.

    D. Add $4.75 for postage and handling.

    E. Figure out the total price for this order.

    F. State that you are enclosing a check or money order for the total payment.

4. Use the correction code sheet on page 26 to proofread and edit your first draft. Make changes and corrections.

5. Write your final draft.

LETTER OF COMPLAINT

Problems often occur on the job. Some of them are easy to solve, but others are not. An employee may have a problem concerning working conditions. A store manager may be dissatisfied with the merchandise ordered from a supplier. In these situations, a letter of complaint can often resolve the problem or at least lead to a compromise settlement.

A letter of complaint should be carefully stated. A letter of complaint provides a written record. It is legally binding and is permanent. Once you put it in writing, you can't "take it back." Therefore, you must choose your words carefully. You must also proofread carefully to correct any errors in grammar or punctuation.

Use this simple two-part format to organize the contents of a letter of complaint:

Paragraph 1:

Give a brief summary of your problem or complaint.

State only the facts as you know them.

I have been scheduled to work for three Saturdays this month. According to the union contract, employees are required to work only one Saturday per month . . .

Paragraph 2:

State what action you would like taken. Be specific.

Perhaps the scheduling problem was an oversight. Please plan my work schedule according to the union contract.

Copy of Letter to a Secondary Person

Sometimes another person is involved in the situation complained about. This person may need to be kept informed about the problem. The writer of the letter should then send the person a copy of the letter. To let the receiver of the letter know this, the writer should write in the left-hand corner below the signature—"cc: (Secondary Person's Name)" for each copy sent.

SAMPLE LETTER OF COMPLAINT

Snappy One Hour Photo Service
1865 Dexter Boulevard
Detroit, MI 48206
July 2, 19__

Mr. Robert Williams,
Commissioner of Public Safety
Detroit Police Department
2056 Woodward Avenue
Detroit, MI 48226

Dear Mr. Williams:

For the past few months, traffic vans have been illegally parking in front of my store. This is a restricted 15-minute parking zone for noncommercial vehicles. There are usually three or four vans parked on the street during business hours. Since I do not have a parking lot, my customers depend on street parking spaces. When I politely asked the van drivers to move their vehicles, they just laughed. When the police pass by, the drivers move their vans and then return within 15 minutes. My business is suffering, since my customers cannot find proper parking space.

I discussed this problem with City Council Member Cynthia Davis, and she suggested that I bring the problem to your attention. I am requesting that you personally investigate this problem and find out why the police are not properly enforcing the parking laws. If this problem is not resolved within ten days of receipt of this letter, I will personally organize the other disgruntled merchants and lead a protest at the next City Council meeting.

I know that I can count on your support. I appreciate your assistance and look forward to hearing from you.

Sincerely,

Maxwell Crowley, Jr.

Maxwell Crowley, Jr.
Manager

cc: Cynthia Davis

❖ Exercise Four

Situation:

You are manager of Sport's World. For a promotion you ordered 500 baseball key chains from L & W Promotions, Inc. When you received your order, you discovered that the company sent you 500 Earth Day key chains. You are sending back the key chains separately by means of United Parcel Service. You want L & W Promotions to send you the key chains that you ordered or refund your $250.00 + $25.75 shipping and handling.

Directions:

Write a business letter to L & W Promotions, Inc., Department 302X, 23450 Memorial Parkway, Dallas, TX 75223. For your inside address, use the following business address: 2046 Bergenline Avenue (Your City, Your State and Zip). Use today's date.

In your letter, be sure to:

1. Use acceptable business letter form. Refer to the style sheet on page 49.

2. Use correct capitalization and punctuation.

3. Write complete sentences in well-developed paragraphs.

   A. In the first paragraph, explain the situation. Include all the facts.

   B. In the second paragraph, state what you want the company to do.

4. Use the correction code sheet on page 26 to proofread and edit your first draft. Make changes and corrections.

5. Write your final draft.

❖ Exercise Five

Situation:

You are employed in the Accounting Department of Creative Graphics, Inc. You worked four hours overtime on Saturday, April 3, 19__ at the request of your supervisor, Enrico Perez. You were supposed to receive overtime pay. On your April 20, 19__ paycheck, you noticed that you did not receive the four hours overtime. You spoke to your supervisor and he suggested that you write a business letter to Ms. Althea Martin, Payroll Supervisor. You want Ms. Martin to correct this error on the next paycheck.

Directions:

Write a business letter to Ms. Althea Martin, Payroll Supervisor, Creative Graphics, Inc., 5764 Houston Street, (Your City, Your State and Zip). Date your letter April 20, 19--.

Be sure to:

1. Use acceptable business letter form.

2. Use correct capitalization and punctuation.

(Exercise continues on the next page)

3. Write complete sentences in well-developed paragraphs.

   A. In the first paragraph, explain the situation. Include all the facts.

   B. In the second paragraph, state what you want the payroll supervisor to do.

4. Send a carbon copy of this letter to your supervisor, Enrico Perez.

5. Use the correction code sheet to help you proofread and edit your first draft. Make changes and corrections.

6. Write your final draft.

LETTER REQUESTING PERMISSION

As an employee, a sudden emergency may occur and you may need to take time off from work. For example, you may need to take a personal day to attend a relative's funeral. Perhaps you need to take a week off to have minor surgery. Maybe you are scheduled to work on a Saturday when you have to attend a wedding. Let's say you first discuss the problem with your supervisor. The supervisor tells you that before any decision can be made, you will have to write a letter requesting permission.

A letter requesting permission can be organized into three short paragraphs.

Paragraph 1:

Describe the problem or situation. Give essential facts and details.

For the past few months, I have been experiencing pain in my left knee. My orthopedic physician recommended that I have minor surgery to correct the problem.

Paragraph 2:

State your request. Be specific.

My physician scheduled me for surgery at Memorial Hospital on June 6, 19--. At his suggestion, I am requesting a two-week sick leave from June 6 until June 20.

Paragraph 3:

Thank the person for assisting you.

I appreciate your assistance.

Copy of Letter to a Secondary Person

If another person is involved, send this person a copy of the letter. To let the receiver of the letter know this, write in the left-hand corner below the signature – "cc: (Secondary Person's Name)" for each carbon copy sent.

SAMPLE LETTER REQUESTING PERMISSION

3063 Calvert Avenue
Apartment 402
Iowa City, Iowa 52248
March 3, 19__

Ms. Carole McDonald,
Personnel Director
Hixby Electronics, Inc.
300 Industrial Drive
Iowa City, Iowa 52243

Dear Ms. McDonald:

I am employed as a stock clerk in the Receiving Department. A serious emergency has occurred and my supervisor, Peter Diaz, recommended that I contact you. Last night, I learned that my brother in Paterson, New Jersey, was in a serious automobile accident. He is now in the hospital in critical condition. Since I am his nearest living relative, I want to be with him at this time.

I am requesting a one-week leave from March 4 until March 11. Mr. Diaz approves my request and assures me that my absence will not upset the department work-load. I would appreciate it if you could let me know before the end of the day so that I can make travel arrangements.

I appreciate your assistance.

Sincerely yours,

Richard Davis

Richard Davis

cc: Peter Diaz

❖ *Exercise Six*

Situation:

You are employed as a salesperson at Wonder World Electronics. You are scheduled to work on the weekend of June 26 and 27 (Saturday and Sunday). On that weekend, you would like to attend your grandparents' 50th wedding anniversary party. The celebration will be held 300 miles from where you live.

Directions:

Write a business letter to Mr. Hector Rodriquez, Manager, Wonder World Electronics, 2030 Route 4, (Your City, Your State and Zip Code). Date the letter June 2, 19__.

In your letter, be sure to:

1. Use acceptable business letter form. Refer to the style sheet on page 49.

2. Use correct capitalization and punctuation.

3. Write complete sentences in well-developed paragraphs.

   A. In the first paragraph, explain the problem. Include all the facts.

   B. In the second paragraph, state your request.

4. Use the correction code sheet on page 26 to proofread and edit your first draft. Make changes and corrections.

5. Write your final draft.

JOB APPLICATION LETTERS, RÉSUMÉS, AND COVER LETTERS

Writing skills are often important in getting a job. Some situations call for an applicant to write a **letter of application.** Or the applicant may be required to send in to the employer a **résumé** with a brief **cover letter.** Each of these requires careful planning.

THE JOB APPLICATION LETTER

A letter of application must look professional and businesslike. If your letter is sloppy or incomplete, the employer will be left with a poor impression about you as a person. To an employer, your letter of application is you.

This lesson will give you the chance to write some sample job application letters. When you write such a letter, make a draft copy. If possible, type the final version. Otherwise, the letter should be neatly handwritten. Never print. Remember: Your letter of application is your introduction to people who could hire you.

A letter applying for a job should include the following:

1. Refer to the job and how you learned about it **(Paragraph 1).**

   I am inquiring about the data-entry clerk position that was advertised in today's Daily News.

2. Provide some information about yourself: the name of your school, courses completed that may relate to the job, etc. **(Paragraph 2).**

   I have taken two years of Word Processing along with Shorthand, Business English, and Principles of Computers.

3. List previous work experience. Explain how it prepared you for the job for which you are applying **(Paragraph 3).**

   During my senior year, I worked as a computer trainee in the Business Coop Program at Globe Insurance Co.

4. List two or three personal references with addresses **(Paragraph 4).**

5. Request an interview **(Paragraph 5).**

   I would be pleased to discuss the job and my qualifications at your convenience.

SAMPLE JOB APPLICATION LETTER

3465 Boulevard East
Apartment 2E
Dallas, TX 75232
May 5, 19__

Fidelity National Bank
P.O. Box 42B
Dallas, TX 75221

Dear Sir or Madam:

(1)   Please consider me as an applicant for the teller trainee position listed in today's Dallas Tribune.

(2)   I am 18 years old. I will graduate from North High School in June. Since my sophomore year, I have been taking business courses. I have taken Accounting 1 and 2, Business Law, Economics, and Word Processing.

(3)   During my junior year, I was in the Co-Op Program in which I attended school one week and worked the alternate week. My work placement was at the Western Insurance Company, where I learned basic accounting procedures. I am currently employed part-time as a cashier at a Pathway Supermarket. These positions helped me to develop skills and confidence for handling large sums of money.

(4)   The following people have given me permission to use their names as references:

    Ms. Marjorie Thompson, Supervisor, Western Insurance Co., 20631 Memorial Parkway, Dallas, TX 75221

    Mr. Roberto Gonzalez, Manager, Pathway Supermarket, 2148 Anderson Avenue, Dallas, TX 75242

    Ms. Betty Wong, Co-Op Coordinator, North High School, 4293 Columbus Avenue, Dallas, TX 75232

(5)   I would be glad to come for an interview at your convenience. My telephone number is 775-2684. I look forward to hearing from you.

Sincerely,

Thomas Gupton

Thomas Gupton

❖ *Exercise One*

Directions:

Write a job application letter. Look in the classified section of the newspaper for a job for which you would like to apply. Attach the ad to the space to the right. Then write a letter of application.

```
┌─ ─ ─ ─ ─ ─ ─ ─ ─ ─ ─ ─ ┐
│                        │
│                        │
│     Attach want ad     │
│     in this space.     │
│                        │
│                        │
└─ ─ ─ ─ ─ ─ ─ ─ ─ ─ ─ ─ ┘
```

Procedures:

1. Use acceptable business letter form. Refer to the style sheet on page 49.

2. Use correct capitalization and punctuation.

3. Write complete sentences in well-developed paragraphs.

   A. In the first paragraph, refer to the job and how you learned about it.

   B. In the second paragraph, include information about yourself—age, name of school, courses completed that may relate to the job.

   C. In the third paragraph, list previous work experience. Explain how it prepared you for the job for which you are applying.

   D. In the fourth paragraph, list three personal references with addresses. Select people who can describe your character or work ability. Teachers, neighbors, and former employers are good choices. Ask permission before using a person's name for a reference.

   E. In the fifth paragraph, request an interview. Include your telephone number.

4. Use the correction code sheet on page 26 to proofread and edit your first draft. Make changes and corrections.

5. Write your final draft.

THE RÉSUMÉ

A personal résumé summarizes information about yourself, your schooling, your background, your work experience, and people to contact as references. A well-prepared résumé can help you get a job. It tells the employer why and how you could be of help on the job. It also saves time—both yours and the employer's.

A résumé should be typed, preferably no more than one page long. It should include:

1. **Personal information:** your full name, address, and phone number.

2. **Education:** schools attended, special courses, and vocational training.

3. **Work experience:** both part- and full-time jobs, including locations and job titles.

4. **Skills and abilities:** equipment you can operate, tasks you know how to perform, specialized knowledge you have, and foreign languages you speak.

5. **Hobbies and interests:** clubs and memberships, sports, special interests like stamp collecting or playing the guitar.

6. **References:** two or three people who know you well and will speak highly of you (do not use parents or relatives).

A COVER LETTER TO GO ALONG WITH THE RÉSUMÉ

When you send a résumé to an employer, you should include a brief "cover" letter. A cover letter is like a job application letter but shorter (since the résumé already covers most of the information you want the employer to know). The cover letter should include:

1. A brief introduction **(Paragraph 1)** that refers to the job and how you learned about it:

   I am writing to inquire about the interior design consultant position that was advertised in this month's Interiors.

2. A very brief summary of information about yourself, especially why you are qualified for the job **(Paragraph 2):**

   I was assistant manager at Multiple Designs, Inc., for the past five years. I created room designs for all styles—traditional to modern. I also worked directly with wholesalers and manufacturers.

3. A concluding statement that expresses interest in the job and the desire for an interview **(Paragraph 3):**

   My work experience and energetic attitude would be a big help to your company. I look forward to meeting you to discuss this position. My résumé is enclosed.

Note: Since you are enclosing your résumé, put the abbreviation **enc.** (enclosure) at the bottom of the page on the left, below the signature.

SAMPLE RÉSUMÉ

—— RÉSUMÉ ——

PERSONAL INFORMATION

Thomas Gupton
1465 Boulevard East
Apartment 2E
Dallas, TX 75232
Phone: (214) 974-3562

EDUCATION

19__ to present. North High School,
4293 Columbus Avenue, Dallas, TX 75232.
Business major. Currently in twelfth grade.

19__ to 19__. Jackson Junior High School,
1034 Houston Avenue, Dallas, TX 75230.
Graduated, June 19__.

WORK EXPERIENCE

19__ to present. Pathway Supermarket,
2148 Anderson Avenue, Dallas, TX 75242. Cashier.

19__ to 19__. Western Insurance Company,
20631 Memorial Parkway, Dallas, TX 75221. Trainee.

SPECIAL ABILITIES

Typing – 60 words per minute, word processing.

HOBBIES AND INTERESTS

Sports – baseball and football.
Collect stamps and baseball cards.

REFERENCES

Ms. Marjorie Thompson, Supervisor, Western Insurance
Company, 20631 Memorial Parkway, Dallas, TX 75221

Mr. Roberto Gonzalez, Manager, Pathway Supermarket,
2148 Anderson Avenue, Dallas, TX 75242

Ms. Betty Wong, Co-Op Coordinator, North High School,
4293 Columbus Avenue, Dallas, TX 75232

SAMPLE COVER LETTER

Study the cover letter that Thomas Gupton sent with his résumé to apply for a job at Citizen's National Bank.

1465 Boulevard East
Apartment 2E
Dallas, TX 75232
May 10, 19__

Citizen's National Bank
P.O. Box 3246
Dallas, TX 75243

Dear Sir or Madam:

I would like to apply for the bank teller position that was advertised in today's Dallas Gazette.

As a senior at North High School, I am completing my senior year in the Business Program with honors. So far, I have earned a 3.8 average.

Enclosed is my résumé. Please telephone me for an interview at your convenience. I look forward to hearing from you.

Sincerely,

Thomas Gupton

Thomas Gupton

enc.

❖ Exercise Two

Situation:

In this exercise, assume you are looking for a job and you are preparing a résumé to help you in your search.

Directions:

1. Prepare a Practice Résumé

A. Write your practice résumé on the next page. Print neatly.

B. Let your teacher correct it.

C. Revise and make final corrections.

2. Prepare Your Final Résumé

A. Type this final version. The form of your résumé should follow the example of the sample résumé on page 68.

B. Proofread and edit your résumé. Use white-out or a correction ribbon to correct errors.

C. Let your teacher correct it.

3. Look for a Job in the Newspaper

A. Find a job in the "want ads" for which you might want to apply. The want ad you choose should request that applicants send in their résumés.

B. Place the want ad in this space.

> **Attach want ad in this space.**

4. Write a Cover Letter.

A. Review the cover letter on page 69.

B. Write a cover letter to the employer. Let your teacher correct it. Make corrections and final changes. Type the final letter.

C. If you want to pursue the job, mail the letter and résumé to the employer.

—— RÉSUMÉ ——

PERSONAL INFORMATION

EDUCATION

WORK EXPERIENCE

SPECIAL ABILITIES

HOBBIES AND INTERESTS

REFERENCES

❖

YOUR OWN PERSONAL DATA SHEET

Forms! Forms! Forms! Wherever you go or whatever you do, you will have to fill out forms. There are many types of forms. *For example:* job application forms, forms you are asked to fill out on the job, hospital and medical forms, insurance forms. Such forms require you to list specific information about yourself, right from your birth on up to the present.

What can happen when you leave out information asked for in a form or fill out the form incorrectly? In the case of a job application, the result might be that you would be eliminated from the applicants who get an interview. Or you might wind up not getting money owed you just because you failed to fill out a required form or filled it out incorrectly. Or you could have trouble with your hospital insurance. Situations like this can be avoided, especially if you have up-to-date information about yourself ready at hand.

GETTING YOUR LIFE TOGETHER

You are an interesting person. You present yourself when you fill out a form. You are in fact telling parts of your life story.

Much of the information that you list on forms is on official records – your birth certificate, religious records, passport, citizenship papers, old school records, etc. You should keep these basic records together in a safe place. The purpose of this unit is to help you get together the facts about yourself that you might be required to list on various forms. You will assemble one group of facts at a time. Then at the end you will put everything together in a full Personal Data Sheet.

GENERAL BACKGROUND INFORMATION

Forms usually begin by asking you to fill out your name, and most forms want you to fill out your *last name first.*

- Put a comma after your last name.

- Then write your first name and middle name or middle initial. Do *not* use nicknames.

You may be asked for your present address *and* your previous address. *Remember:* Your previous address is where you lived before you moved to your present address. For each address, be sure to include the number and street and the zip code.

You may be asked for the date of your birth and the place of your birth. Usually in answer to the latter question you will only have to list the city and state or province and the country (such as U.S. or Canada or Mexico or Japan). Are you a U.S. citizen? The form may ask you this. And if you are not, the form may ask you for your Alien Registration Number.

Do you have a Social Security number? You will be asked for it over and over again. If you don't have a Social Security number, get one. *(See Unit Nine.)*

You know the meaning of the term *marital status.* You should be able to answer any question regarding this.

Some forms ask you if you have any physical handicaps. If you do, describe them accurately.

Finally, some forms ask you information about your parents – their names, you mother's maiden name, and their occupations. And some forms ask you whom to notify in case of emergency. This is usually your mother or father or some other close relative. List the name and his or her address (including street address and zip code) and a telephone number where this person can be reached.

Turn the page and begin getting information together for your own Personal Data Sheet.

❖ Exercise One

Directions:

Fill in the information below.

Name _____ _____
      LAST   FIRST   MIDDLE   TELEPHONE NO.

Present Address _____
      NO.   STREET   CITY   STATE (PROVINCE) ZIP

Previous Address _____
      NO.   STREET   CITY   STATE (PROVINCE) ZIP

Date of Birth _____
      MONTH   DAY   YEAR

Place of Birth _____
      CITY   STATE (PROVINCE)   COUNTRY

Are You a U.S. Citizen? ☐ Yes ☐ No

If not, what is your Alien Registration No.? _____

Social Security No. _____

Marital Status _____

List Any Physical Handicaps _____

Father's Name _____

Mother's Name _____

Mother's Maiden Name _____

Father's Occupation _____

Mother's Occupation _____

In Case of Emergency, Notify _____
      NAME

_____
ADDRESS   TELEPHONE NO.

EDUCATION HISTORY

A second type of information which job applications and other forms are likely to ask of you is your education history. You are unlikely to have in your memory all the information you may need about each school you attended. Get the facts straight and for each school, list:

1. Official name of school

2. Address – number, street, city, state and zip

3. Date started (month and year)

4. Date graduated or left (month and year)

5. Grade completed

6. Course of study – business, vocational, co-op, general, etc.

What if you attended more than one junior high school or high school? Simple. Just list the required information for the last school attended.

❖ Exercise Two

Directions:

Now see if you can correctly describe your education history below.

	EDUCATION RECORD					
Type of School	Name of School	Address	Date Started	Date Left	Grade Completed	Course of Study
Elementary						
Junior High School						
High School						
Other						

PERSONAL WORK EXPERIENCE

The next type of information that you are likely to need concerns your personal work experience. Start with your most recent job. For each of your jobs, you should be able to list the following:

1. Name of employer

2. Address — number, street, city, state and zip code

3. Date hired

4. Date left

5. Salary

6. Reason for leaving — laid-off, quit, new job, etc.

7. Supervisor's name. This is the person you reported to or who was in charge of your department.

❖ Exercise Three

Directions:

Now, see if you can correctly summarize your personal work experience below. (*Note:* Some of you are still in school and may never have had a paying job. If this is true of you, ask yourself if you ever did volunteer work. If so, list it here.)

PERSONAL WORK EXPERIENCE						
(List below last three employers. Start with last one first.)						
Name of Employer	Address	Job Title	Date Hired	Date Left	Last Salary	Reason for Leaving

JOB SKILLS

Do you have any special job skills? Do you know how to operate any machines?

When you answer questions about job skills, it is better to be specific. For example, if you know WordPerfect, it is better to list *WordPerfect* than it is to simply list *Word Processing*. If you type 50 words per minute, it is better to answer *Type 50 w.p.m.* than it is to simply answer *Type*.

❖ Exercise Four

Directions:

List your job skills.

Machines Operated _____

_____

Other Job Skills _____

_____

PERSONAL REFERENCES

Job application forms usually ask you to list two or three personal references, that is, responsible adults who can honestly describe your character and work skills. Unfortunately, you cannot list your relatives as references. Then who can you list? Possible choices are a neighbor, a teacher, a former employer, or a minister or priest. Get their permission before you use their names for references.

You must be able to list the following information for each personal reference:

1. Full name

2. Address – number, street, city, state and zip code

3. Occupation – the type of work the person does to earn a living

4. How long you have known this person

5. The person's phone number

❖ Exercise Five

Directions:

Now list your personal references below.

PERSONAL REFERENCES (Do not list the names of relatives.)				
Name	Address	Occupation	Years Known	Phone No.

Congratulations! You have just gathered together important information for filling out application forms, job forms, medical records, insurance claims, and many other types of forms.

❖ Exercise Six

Directions:

To make sure that you have this information ready for use whenever you need it, fill out the Personal Data Sheet which begins on the next page. It will summarize on one sheet (front and back) all the information from all the previous exercises.

After you fill out the Personal Data Sheet, proofread and edit it. Make a duplicate copy and put it away in a safe place for future use. Take the original copy with you whenever you are likely to have to fill out forms. Your Personal Data Sheet should make filling out these forms an easy task.

PERSONAL DATA SHEET

This PERSONAL DATA SHEET contains important information which you should have at hand when you fill out job applications or other forms. Keep the Personal Data Sheet in your wallet or purse.

Name _____
       LAST   FIRST   MIDDLE   TELEPHONE NO.

Present Address _____
       NO.   STREET   CITY   STATE (PROVINCE) ZIP

Previous Address _____
       NO.   STREET   CITY   STATE (PROVINCE) ZIP

Date of Birth _____
       MONTH   DAY   YEAR

Place of Birth _____
       CITY   STATE (PROVINCE)   COUNTRY

Are You a U.S. Citizen? ☐ Yes ☐ No

If not, what is your Alien Registration No.? _____

Social Security No. _____

Marital Status _____

List Any Physical Handicaps _____

Father's Name _____

Mother's Name _____

Mother's Maiden Name _____

Father's Occupation _____

Mother's Occupation _____

In Case of Emergency, Notify _____
                NAME

_____
ADDRESS   TELEPHONE NO.

(Personal Data Sheet continued on the next page)

EDUCATION RECORD

Type of School	Name of School	Address	Date Started	Date Left	Grade Completed	Course of Study
Elementary						
Junior High School						
High School						
Other						

PERSONAL WORK EXPERIENCE
(List below last three employers. Start with last one first.)

Name of Employer	Address	Job Title	Date Hired	Date Left	Last Salary	Reason for Leaving

Machines Operated _____

_____

Other Job Skills _____

_____

PERSONAL REFERENCES
(Do not list the names of relatives.)

Name	Address	Occupation	Years Known	Phone No.

JOB APPLICATION FORMS

First impressions are important. This is especially true when a person applies for a job. And a job application is often a first impression. It allows an employer to get to know the job applicant. If the application is filled out correctly, the applicant will make a good impression. If it is filled out sloppily, an employer may feel that the applicant would be a sloppy worker.

There are usually too many applicants for any available job. An employer cannot interview every applicant. The employer selects applicants to interview from their job applications. An applicant who fills out an application correctly has a better chance for an interview. A sloppy application will not be considered.

The exercises in this unit will prepare you to fill out job applications completely, accurately, and neatly.

RULES FOR FILLING OUT A JOB APPLICATION

Here are important rules for filling out a job application.

1. Type or print neatly with blue or black ink.

2. Bring a pen with you if you plan to fill out an application at a company.

3. Spell all words correctly. Write difficult words out in advance on a sheet of paper and have this sheet with you when you fill out the application.

4. Fill in all information. You must know the names and addresses of:
   - the schools you attended
   - your previous employers
   - your personal references

   This information should be on your Personal Data Sheet.

5. Do not put false information on the application.

   Employers do check the accuracy of employment forms. Putting false information on a job application is cause for an employer to fire you.

AN EXAMPLE OF A GOOD JOB OF FILLING OUT A JOB APPLICATION

Look at the application on pages 83 and 84. The applicant filled it out completely and accurately. If you read it carefully, you will see that she has good job qualifications and has had previous job experience. Chances are that she will be considered for a job interview.

❖ Exercise One

As you read through the application on pages 83 and 84, you should be able to answer the following questions.

1. What is the applicant's <u>last</u> name? _____

2. The form asked her to list her age if she was under 18. It appears she was

   a. under 18

   b. over 18

3. What is the relationship of Mary Gomez to the applicant? _____

4. Does the applicant have any relatives working for the company? _____

5. What is the zip code of the applicant's grammar school? _____

6. When she left the Shopping Center, what was her salary per hour? _____

7. What is the name of her business teacher whom she listed as a reference? _____

8. What was the date when she submitted this application? _____

APPLICATION FOR EMPLOYMENT

PERSONAL DATA

PLEASE TYPE OR PRINT CLEARLY

Position Applied For	Date	Social Security Number
Word Processor	7-7-1991	232-95-4111

Date of Birth (if under 18) _____

Mr./Ms./Mrs. <u>Gomez ,</u>   <u>Evelyn</u>   <u>R.</u>
            LAST   FIRST   MIDDLE

Address <u>145 Trinity Place, Apt. 37A New York,   NY   10025 (212) 928-3982</u>
         NUMBER & STREET   CITY   STATE   ZIP   TELEPHONE

Check One: ☑ U.S. Citizen ☐ Permanent Resident Alien Card # _____

Have You Ever Been Convicted Of A Felony? ☐ Yes ☑ No
If Yes, Explain _____

Have You Any Physical Defects Which Preclude You From Performing Certain Kinds of Work? ☐ Yes ☑ No If Yes, Explain _____

Have You Ever Applied to This Company Before? ☐ Yes ☑ No
If Yes, Explain _____

Name of Relatives Employed by This Company <u>none</u>

In Case of Emergency, Notify <u>Mary Gomez</u>   <u>Mother</u>
                    NAME   RELATIONSHIP

<u>145 Trinity Place, Apt. 37A   New York, NY   10025   (212) 928-3982</u>
ADDRESS   TELEPHONE

EDUCATION

TYPE OF SCHOOL	NAME & ADDRESS	YEARS ATTENDED	DATE GRADUATED
Grammar	JH 78, 2141 Columbus Ave. New York, NY 10023	3	6-24-87
High School	J.F. Kennedy High School 122 W. 76th St., New York, NY 10025	3	6-29-90
College	N.Y. College of Office Knowledge 47 W. 13th St., New York, NY 10011	YRS. ATT. 1 DATE GRAD. 6-21-91	COURSE OF STUDY Secretarial Studies

FORM CONTINUES ON THE NEXT PAGE

WORK SKILLS

What Kind(s) Of Work Can You Do? _Word Processor, WordPerfect_

What Machines Can You Operate? _IBM Cash Register_ Typing Speed _60 w.p.m._

Shorthand Speed _50 w.p.m._

PREVIOUS WORK EXPERIENCE

(List Below Previous Three Employers. Start With Last One First.)

May We Call Your Present Empolyer? ☐ Yes ☐ No

NAME OF EMPLOYER	ADDRESS	JOB TITLE	NAME OF SUPERVISOR	DATES EMPLOYED	LAST SALARY	REASON FOR LEAVING
North American Insurance Co.	4060 Madison Ave. New York, NY 10024	Word Processor	James Rooney	6/90 - 9/91	$6.25 hour	Co-Op Job
Shopping Center	1092 Third Ave. New York, NY 10022	Cashier	Jane Wiggins	7/89 - 6/90	$4.50 hour	New Job

PERSONAL REFERENCES

(List Below Three Refernces, Other Than Relatives Or Former Employers.)

NAME	ADDRESS	OCCUPATION	YEARS KNOWN	PHONE NO.
Ms. Helene Williams	J.F. Kennedy High School 122 W. 76th St., NY, NY 10025	Business Teacher	3	(212) 941-8700 Ext. 27
Mr. John Rossi	J.F. Kennedy High School 122 W. 76th St., NY, NY 10025	Counselor	3	(212) 941-8700 Ext. 82
Ms. Ann Johnson	145 Trinity Place, Apt.26B New York, NY 10025	Manager Clothing Store	6	(212) 782-5521

I authorize investigation of all statements contained in this application.
I understand that misrepresentation or omission of facts is cause for dismissal.

Date _July 7, 1991_ Signature _Evelyn Gomez_

AN EXAMPLE OF A POOR JOB OF FILLING OUT A JOB APPLICATION

Next, look at the application on page 86. The applicant did not fill out the application completely or accurately. He left out important information. He may not have had a Personal Data Sheet on hand. Chances are that the applicant will not be considered for a job interview.

❖ Exercise Two

Directions:

Try to identify the errors Mr. Atherton made in filling out his application.

1. How should Mr. Atherton have listed his name? (Follow the form's instructions, and do <u>not</u> include his nickname.)

_____
   LAST   **FIRST**   **MIDDLE**

2. What part of his address was left out on Line 2? _____

3. What is the error on Line 4? _____

4. What errors did he make on Lines 5 and 6? _____

5. In his record of previous employment, which listing contains an incomplete address?

    a. Line 9

    b. Line 10

6. What did he leave out on Line 10? _____

7. What did he leave out in the address on Line 13? _____

8. Line 13 is also messy. Why? _____

9. What did he leave out on Line 15? _____

10. What is the error on Line 17? _____

11. What is the error on Line 18? _____

12. What is the error on Line 19? _____

APPLICATION FOR EMPLOYMENT

(1) Name **Atherton** (LAST) **Robert** (FIRST) "Sonny" **J** (MIDDLE) Age **17**

(2) Address **3062 Webb Ave.** Phone **234-1892**

(3) No. of years residing at the above address **5 yrs.** Social Security No. **289-487-25□**

(4) Check one: ☐ U.S. Citizen ☐ Permanent Resident Alien Card No. _____

(5) Have you ever been convicted of a felony? _____

(6) If so, explain _____

(7) Position Applied for **Mail Room Clerk** Salary Desired **$5 per hour**

(8) Part or Full-Time **Full** Hours per week you can work **40 per week**

RECORD OF PREVIOUS EXPERIENCE

	From	To	Name of Firm	Address	Position Held	Reason for Leaving
(9)	6/3/92		Gateway Supermarket	Chicago, Il 60602	Cashier	Still employed
(10)	3/3/91		Service	4063 Clark St., Chicago, Il 60602		
(11)						
(12)						

EDUCATION RECORD – List Last Three Schools Attended

	Name of School	Address	Phone No.	Course of Study	Grade Completed
(13)	Grant Elementary	4063 Kay St., Chicago, Il	288-3651	General	6th
(14)	Lincoln Jr. High	3112 Deonoster Ave, Chicago, Il 60626	918-3465	General	9th
(15)	Washington High School	2004 West St., Chicago, Il 60614		Business	10th

REFERENCES – (Other than Relatives, Personal Physician, or Clergyman)

	Name	Address	Phone No.	Occupation	Years Known
(16)	Ms. Olive Johnson	2004 West St. Chicago, Il 60614	841-1800	Counselor	3 yrs.
(17)	Mr. Juan Deleon	2001 West St. Chicago, Il 60617	841-1500		2 yrs.
(18)	Mr. Alex James	4034 Berry Ave Chicago, Il 60621	321-2414	Manager	

I CERTIFY THAT THE INFORMATION GIVEN ABOVE IS CORRECT TO THE BEST OF MY KNOWLEDGE AND GIVE THIS COMPANY THE AUTHORIZATION TO INQUIRE ABOUT ME, AND BOND ME IF HIRED. I UNDERSTAND THAT MISREPRESENTATION OR OMISSION OF FACTS IS CAUSE FOR DISMISSAL.

I WILL ABIDE BY ALL RULES, REGULATIONS AND POLICIES OF THIS COMPANY.

(19) Date _____ , 19 _____ *Robert "Sonny" J. Atherton*
SIGNATURE OF APPLICANT

IMPORTANT: IF YOU ARE UNDER 18 YEARS OF AGE, WORKING PAPERS MUST BE SUBMITTED BEFORE HIRING.

DOCUMENTS YOU MAY NEED WHEN YOU MAKE YOUR APPLICATION

When you apply for a job, you will want to take along your Personal Data Sheet. You may need proof of citizenship. Or, if you are a resident alien, you may need your Permanent Resident Alien Card. If you are under age, you may need working papers.

SPECIAL QUESTIONS YOU MAY HAVE TO ANSWER

Included in the questions you may have to answer are such things as the following:

1. How were you referred to this company?

Did you see an ad? (If so describe it.) Did a friend refer you? Is this friend an employee of the company? (If so, say, *"Referred by friend who is employee."* Or name the person.) Did a school counselor suggest you apply? (If so, say so.) Or did you decide on your own initiative? (If so, write *"On my own."*)

2. Salary required.

How much is the job likely to pay? Is that satisfactory to you? Don't put too low a figure down. Doing this won't give you an edge. But don't put down an amount that is more than the employer will probably want to pay.

3. Hobbies, special interests, and activities.

What kinds of hobbies and special interests do you have? What kinds of extracurricular activities did you take part in in school? What sports do you like?

You don't have to list everything. The most important things to list are things that may be relevant to the job. *For example:* Tinkering with cars if you are applying for a mechanic's job. Or reading if you are applying for a job in a library.

Be sure you list any activities you take part in that are a part of public service. *For example:* Being a member of a volunteer fire department, or helping with a youth group or with senior citizens. And do list the interests and hobbies that are really important to you.

HOW TO LIST DATES

The simplest way to list dates—and the way that takes up the least space—is by numbers. *For example:* 2-13-93. (This means February 13, 1993.)

- **The first number is for the month.**

    Feb. = 2

    July = 7

    Oct. = 10

- **The next number is for the day of the month.**

    Feb. 7   =   2-7

    Oct. 25   =   10-25

    April 1   =   4-1

- **The last number is for the year. (But only list the last 2 digits.)**

    June 23, 1995 = 6-23-95

    Sept. 8, 1976 = 9-8-76

    Jan. 19, 1997 = 1-19-97

❖ Exercise Three

Directions:

Answer the following questions regarding dates.

1. Spell out the month, the day, and the year for each of the following.

    a. 5-29-92   = May 29, 1992

    b. 11-7-90   = _____ 7, _____

    c. 12-23-86 = _____ _____ , _____

    d. 8-24-89   = _____ _____ , _____

2. Write out the following dates, using numbers.

    a. June 14, 1994   = _____ – _____ – _____

    b. March 3, 1975   = _____ – _____ – _____

    c. September 20, 1991 = _____ – _____ – _____

    d. January 3, 1986   = _____ – _____ – _____

3. A form asks the dates Pascual attended his vocational school. He was there from September 1990 to June 1992. Fill in these dates, using numbers. Note that in this case you only have to list the month and year for each date, <u>not</u> the day of the month.

    From: _____   To: _____

STATEMENTS THAT APPEAR ON APPLICATION FORMS

The unit on vocabulary introduced some of the special statements that appear on application forms. A thought to remember: ***Never sign any document unless you understand what it says.***

❖ Exercise Four

Directions:

In simple language, explain what each of the following statements means. Use a dictionary if you have to, or refer back to *Unit Four*.

1. I will abide by the rules, regulations, and policies of this company.

   _____

   _____

   _____

2. Selection of employees will be on the basis of occupational qualifications, education, and character without regard to age, sex, race, creed, color, or national origin.

   _____

   _____

   _____

   _____

   _____

   Which of the following will the company take into account when hiring?

   a. the fact that an applicant is a Baptist

   b. the fact that an applicant was born in Mexico

   c. the work skills of an applicant

3. I certify that the information given is correct to the best of my knowledge and give this company the authorization to inquire about me, and bond me if hired.

_____

_____

_____

_____

_____

_____

_____

Would you sign a form that said this? _____

4. I understand that misrepresentation or omission of facts is cause for dismissal.

_____

_____

SAMPLE APPLICATION FORMS FOR YOU TO PRACTICE ON

The job application forms on the pages that follow are similar to the job application forms you will fill out when you apply for jobs.

❖ Exercise Five

Directions:

Refer to your Personal Data Sheet as you complete each application. Write neatly and clearly. Be careful about your spelling. Be sure to answer all of the questions that apply to you.

RESTAURANT OPERATIONS
HOURLY EMPLOYEE

APPLICATION FOR EMPLOYMENT

Burger King Corporation

AN EQUAL OPPORTUNITY EMPLOYER — M/F/H

Discrimination in employment because of race, creed, color, national origin, ancestry, age, sex, physical or mental handicaps, or liability for service in the armed forces of the U.S. is prohibited by federal legislation and/or by laws against discrimination in some states.

EDUCATION

LAST NAME	FIRST	MIDDLE INITIAL	PHONE
STREET ADDRESS	CITY	STATE	ZIP CODE

SOCIAL SECURITY NUMBER

NAME AND PHONE OF PERSON TO BE NOTIFIED FOR EMERGENCY
(Do not answer in New York State)

KNOWN PHYSICAL DEFECTS WHICH COULD AFFECT YOUR ABILITY TO PERFORM POSITION BEING APPLIED FOR:

IS YOUR CITIZENSHIP OR IMMIGRATION STATUS SUCH THAT YOU CAN LAWFULLY WORK IN THE U.S.? ☐ YES ☐ NO
IF HIRED, CONTINUED EMPLOYMENT MAY BE DEPENDENT UPON PROOF OF CITIZENSHIP OR PRESENTATION OF AN ALIEN REGISTRATION NUMBER.

ARE YOU: ☐ 14-15 ☐ 16-17 ☐ 18 OR OLDER   IF UNDER 18, PROOF OF AGE MUST BE PROVIDED PRIOR TO HIRING

PERSONAL

NAME OF SCHOOL AND ADDRESS	DATES FROM (Mo./Yr.)	TO (Mo./Yr.)	GRADUATED YES	NO	NUMBER OF COLLEGE CREDIT HOURS	MAJOR	AVERAGE
JUNIOR HIGH							
HIGH SCHOOL							
COLLEGE							
OTHER							

EXTRACURRICULAR ACTIVITIES	CURRENTLY ENROLLED IN HIGH SCHOOL WORKS/STUDY PROGRAM ☐ YES ☐ **NO**

GENERAL ACTIVITIES

DATE AVAILABLE TO START

WHAT INTERESTED YOU IN BURGER KING?

WHAT ARE YOUR HOBBIES, SPECIAL INTEREST, AND ACTIVITIES?
(Do not include those indicating race, creed, nationality or religion)

DO NOT ANSWER THE FOLLOWING QUESTION IN NEW YORK STATE OR MASSACHUSETTS OR — IF CONVICTION OCCURRED MORE THAN SEVEN (7) YEARS AGO — IN WASHINGTON STATE. A RECORD OR CONVICTION DOES NOT DISQUALIFY YOU FROM EMPLOYMENT CONSIDERATION.

HAVE YOU EVER BEEN CONVICTED OF A FELONY OR MISDEMEANOR OTHER THAN A TRAFFIC VIOLATION   ☐ YES ☐ NO
IF YES, STATE CHARGE, COURT, DATE AND DISPOSITION OF CASE

EMPLOYMENT WORK EXPERIENCE

COMPANY NO. 1 (Present or most recent employer)		ADDRESS/PHONE NUMBER	
EMPLOYED (Month & Year) FROM TO	RATE OF PAY START ENDING		AVERAGE NUMBER OF HOURS WORKED PER WEEK
POSITION(S) HELD		SUPERVISOR'S NAME/POSITION	
DESCRIBE YOUR DUTIES			
MAY WE CONTACT THIS EMPLOYER? ☐ YES ☐ NO	DAYS LOST FROM WORK (Do not answer in New York State)		
REASON FOR LEAVING			

COMPANY NO. 2		ADDRESS/PHONE NUMBER	
EMPLOYED (Month & Year) FROM TO	RATE OF PAY START ENDING		AVERAGE NUMBER OF HOURS WORKED PER WEEK
POSITION(S) HELD		SUPERVISOR'S NAME/POSITION	
DESCRIBE YOUR DUTIES			
MAY WE CONTACT THIS EMPLOYER? ☐ YES ☐ NO	DAYS LOST FROM WORK (Do not answer in New York State)		
REASON FOR LEAVING			

THE IMFORMATION I AM PRESENTING IN THIS APPLICATION IS TRUE AND CORRECT TO THE BEST OF MY KNOWLEDGE, AND I UNDERSTAND THAT **ANY** FALSIFICATION OR MISREPRESENTATION HEREIN COULD RESULT IN MY DISCHARGE IN THE EVENT I AM EMPLOYED BY THE BURGER KING CORP-ORATION. I AUTHORIZE BURGER KING CORPORATION OR ITS REPRESENTATIVES TO CONTACT ALL FORMER EMPLOYERS AND TO FURTHER INQUIRE **AS** TO ANY IMFORMATION GIVEN BY ME ON THIS APPLICATION.

APPLICANT'S SIGNATURE _____ DATE _____

DO NOT WRITE BELOW THIS LINE — FOR BURGER KING RESTAURANT USE ONLY

COMPANY NO. 1 REFERENCE CHECK			GOOD	AVERAGE	POOR
APPLICANT ELIGIBLE FOR REHIRE:	☐ YES ☐ NO	ATTENDANCE:	☐	☐	☐
DATES OF EMPLOYMENT VERIFIED:	☐ YES ☐ NO	PERFORMANCE:	☐	☐	☐

CHECKED BY:	CONTACTED:	DATE

COMPANY NO. 2 REFERENCE CHECK			GOOD	AVERAGE	POOR
APPLICANT ELIGIBLE FOR REHIRE:	☐ YES ☐ NO	ATTENDANCE:	☐	☐	☐
DATES OF EMPLOYMENT VERIFIED:	☐ YES ☐ NO	PERFORMANCE:	☐	☐	☐

CHECKED BY:	CONTACTED:	DATE

MANAGER'S/INTERVIEWER'S NOTES:

APPLICATION FOR EMPLOYMENT

WAKEFERN FOOD CORPORATION

SHOP-RITE SUPERMARKETS

DATE _____   SOCIAL SECURITY NUMBER

LAST NAME _____   FIRST NAME _____   INITIAL _____

STREET NO. _____ STREET NAME _____ CITY _____ STATE _____ ZIP _____ TELEPHONE NO. _____

POSITION APPLYING FOR: 1. _____   2. _____   SALARY REQUIRED _____

WHO WERE YOU REFERRED BY? _____

HAVE YOU EVER WORKED FOR WAKEFERN/SHOP-RITE?   YES _____ NO _____ WHEN? _____

WHERE? _____

NAMES OF RELATIVES EMPLOYED BY WAKEFERN/SHOP-RITE _____

ARE YOU A CITIZEN OF THE U.S.A.?   YES _____ NO _____ IF NOT, LIST REGISTRATION NUMBER _____

EDUCATIONAL BACKGROUND	NAME AND ADDRESS	YEARS ATTENDED	GRADUATED	COURSE OR MAJOR
HIGH SCHOOL			☐ Yes ☐ No	
COLLEGE			☐ Yes ☐ No	
BUSINESS OR TRADE			☐ Yes ☐ No	
OTHER			☐ Yes ☐ No	

MILITARY SERVICE RECORD	Have you ever served in the armed forces? ☐ Yes ☐ No	If not, wny?

DATES OF DUTY:
FROM _____ Month _____ Day _____ Year _____ TO _____ Month _____ Day _____ Year   RANK AT DISCHARGE

ANY JOB RELATED EXPERIENCE?

IN CASE OF EMERGENCY NOTIFY: _____ TELEPHONE: _____

ADDRESS: _____

_____ Relationship _____

PRIOR WORK HISTORY (LIST IN ORDER, LAST OR PRESENT EMPLOYER FIRST)

	DATES		NAME AND ADDRESS OF EMPLOYER	RATE OF PAY		SUPERVISOR'S NAME AND TITLE	REASON FOR LEAVING
	FROM	TO		START	FINISH		
1							

DESCRIBE IN DETAIL THE WORK YOU DID.

	DATES		NAME AND ADDRESS OF EMPLOYER	RATE OF PAY		SUPERVISOR'S NAME AND TITLE	REASON FOR LEAVING
	FROM	TO		START	FINISH		
2							
	DESCRIBE IN DETAIL THE WORK YOU DID.						
3							
	DESCRIBE IN DETAIL THE WORK YOU DID.						
4							
	DESCRIBE IN DETAIL THE WORK YOU DID.						

AGREEMENT

1. I AGREE AND UNDERSTAND THAT ALL THE STATEMENTS AND INFORMATION ON MY APPLICATION ARE CORRECT AND NO ATTEMPT HAS BEEN MADE TO CONCEAL OR WITHHOLD PERTINENT INFORMATION. I AGREE THAT ANY OMISSION, FALSIFICATION, OR MISREPRESENTATION IS CAUSE FOR IMMEDIATE TERMINATION AT ANY TIME DURING MY EMPLOYMENT.

2. WITH THE EXCEPTION OF MY CURRENT EMPLOYER, I HEREBY AUTHORIZE INVESTIGATION OF ALL STATEMENTS AT THIS TIME WITH NO LIABILITY ARISING THEREFROM.

3. I WILL ABIDE BY ALL RULES, REGULATIONS AND POLICIES OF WAKEFERN/SHOP-RITE.

4. AT THE OPTION OF THE COMPANY, I AGREE TO A PHYSICAL EXAMINATION BY A PHYSICIAN CHOSEN BY WAKEFERN/SHOP-RITE WITH THE UNDERSTANDING THAT MY EMPLOYMENT AT WAKEFERN/SHOP-RITE DEPENDS UPON MY PASSING THE PHYSICAL.

_____   _____
DATE   SIGNATURE

DO NOT WRITE BELOW THIS LINE

START DATE	STORE/DEPARTMENT (NAME & NO.)		SHIFT	RATE/SALARY
JOB TITLE	EMPLOYEE NUMBER	PART TIME/FULL TIME	DATE OF BIRTH	HEIGHT_____ WEIGHT _____

MARITAL STATUS_____ SINGLE_____ MARRIED _____ SEPARATED_____ DIVORCED

_____ WIDOWED _____ ENGAGED _____ NUMBER OF CHILDREN

WORKING PAPERS ☐ YES ☐ NO

Interviewed by

REMARKS:

_____
_____
_____

N.I.	P.	Sent	

DUNKIN' DONUTS

APPLICATION FOR EMPLOYMENT
IN THE WORLD'S LARGEST AND FINEST
CHAIN OF COFFEE AND DONUT SHOPS

NAME _____ DATE _____

ADDRESS _____ TELEPHONE NUMBER _____

CITY & STATE _____ SOCIAL SECURITY NUMBER _____
(ZIP CODE)

HIGH SCHOOL _____ COLLEGE _____

CITY & STATE _____ CITY & STATE _____

LAST YEAR COMPLETED _____ LAST YEAR COMPLETED _____

EXTRA-CURRICULAR ACTIVITIES (CLUBS, HOBBIES, ORGANIZATIONS) _____

_____

HOW WERE YOU REFERRED TO DUNKIN' DONUTS? _____

EARNINGS EXPECTED PER HOUR: _____ PER WEEK: _____

EMPLOYMENT RECORD
(LIST MOST RECENT EMPLOYMENT FIRST)

NAME AND ADDRESS OF COMPANY	DATE TO - FROM	TYPE WORK	SALARY	NAME OF SUPERVISOR	REASON FOR LEAVING

AVAILABILITY - STATE ALL HOURS YOU WILL BE ABLE TO WORK IN CHART BELOW

	MONDAY	TUESDAY	WEDNESDAY	THURSDAY	FRIDAY	SATURDAY	SUNDAY	CHECK ONE
FROM								☐ FULL TIME
TO								☐ PART TIME

IMPORTANT: IF YOU ARE UNDER 18 YEARS OF AGE, WORKING PAPERS MUST BE SUBMITTED BEFORE HIRING

Please read the following statement and circle the appropriate response:

YES   NO   If a job opportunity is offered, I shall comply with all Dunkin' Donuts' uniform requirements. I understand that job responsibilities often include counter work, donut preparation and cleaning duties.

The facts set forth in my application for employment are true and complete. I understand that if I am employed, false statements on this application shall be considered sufficient cause for dismissal.

_____
SIGNATURE OF APPLICANT

Selection of employees will be on the basis of occupational qualification, education and character without regard to age, sex, race, creed, color or national origin.

PER/115/Rev 1/80

APPLYING FOR A SOCIAL SECURITY CARD

Before you begin work on almost any job, you must have a Social Security card. A Social Security card is easy to get. Just fill out an application, **Form SS-5**, completely and accurately (see the copy to practice on on page 98). Here are situations when you will need to fill out this form.

1. **If you have never had a Social Security card.** Along with a completed application form, you must include documents, such as a birth certificate, that show your age, citizenship, and who you are.

2. **If you need to replace your card.** Along with the completed application form, you must include one type of identification.

3. **If you need to change your name on the card.** Along with the completed application form, you must include a document that identifies you both by your old name and your new name. *For example:* A marriage certificate, a divorce decree, or a court order that changes your name.

4. **If you apply for a card for your child.** You must answer the questions on the application form as they apply to the child. Then you sign your name under number 16 and check the correct box in number 17. You will need identification that shows who you are. You will also need the child's birth certificate and one more document that shows the child's identity.

Here are the types of documents that show Social Security who you are:

- Driver's license

- Your passport

- School records
  (ID card or report card)

- Health insurance card

- Insurance policy

- Adoption records

- Military records

- Court order for name change

- Religious records

- Any other document that establishes your identity

Social Security only accepts original documents or certified copies. A photocopy of a document can be certified by the County Clerk or the person who keeps the records.

CAUTION: If you mail official documents, they can be lost or stolen. A good thing to do is to go to the Post Office and send your documents by *certified mail* with a request for a *return receipt.* The return receipt will tell you who actually received your package. The cost of certified return receipt mail is about $2.

Another possibility is to bring the documents directly to your nearest Social Security office, if there is one near you.

Filling out an application for a Social Security card is easy. If you have any questions, call 1-(800)-234-5772 or your nearest Social Security office.

❖ *Exercise One*

Directions:

Fill out the application for a Social Security Card **(Form SS-5)** on the next page.

SOCIAL SECURITY ADMINISTRATION
Application for a Social Security Card

Form Approved
OMB No. 0960-0066

INSTRUCTIONS

- Please read "How To Complete This Form" on page 2.
- Print or type using black or blue ink. DO NOT USE PENCIL.
- After you complete this form, take or mail it along with the required documents to your nearest Social Security office.
- If you are completing this form for someone else, answer the questions as they apply to that person. Then, sign your name in question 16.

1 NAME
To Be Shown On Card

▶ _____
FIRST   FULL MIDDLE NAME   LAST

FULL NAME AT BIRTH
IF OTHER THAN ABOVE
_____
FIRST   FULL MIDDLE NAME   LAST

OTHER NAMES USED _____

2 MAILING ADDRESS
Do Not Abbreviate

▶ _____
STREET ADDRESS, APT. NO., PO BOX, RURAL ROUTE NO.

_____
CITY   STATE   ZIP CODE

3 CITIZENSHIP
(Check One)

☐ U.S. Citizen ☐ Legal Alien Allowed To Work ☐ Legal Alien Not Allowed To Work ☐ Foreign Student Allowed Restricted Employment ☐ Conditionally Legalized Alien Allowed To Work ☐ Other (See Instructions On Page 2)

4 SEX

☐ Male ☐ Female

5 RACE/ETHNIC DESCRIPTION
(Check One Only—Voluntary)

☐ Asian, Asian-American Or Pacific Islander ☐ Hispanic ☐ Black (Not Hispanic) ☐ North American Indian Or Alaskan Native ☐ White (Not Hispanic)

6 DATE OF BIRTH _____
MONTH DAY YEAR

7 PLACE OF BIRTH
(Do Not Abbreviate) _____ CITY   STATE OR FOREIGN COUNTRY

| | Office Use Only |
| FCI | |

8 MOTHER'S MAIDEN NAME
_____
FIRST   FULL MIDDLE NAME   LAST NAME AT HER BIRTH

9 FATHER'S NAME
_____
FIRST   FULL MIDDLE NAME   LAST

10 Has the person in item 1 ever applied for or received a Social Security number before?

☐ Yes (If "yes", answer questions 11-13.)   ☐ No (If "no", go on to question 14.)   ☐ Don't Know (If "don't know", go on to question 14.)

11 Enter the Social Security number previously assigned to the person listed in item 1.

☐☐☐ – ☐☐ – ☐☐☐☐

12 Enter the name shown on the most recent Social Security card issued for the person listed in item 1.

_____
FIRST   MIDDLE   LAST

13 Enter any different date of birth if used on an earlier application for a card. _____
MONTH   DAY   YEAR

14 TODAY'S DATE ▶ _____   **15 DAYTIME PHONE NUMBER** ▶ (___)
MONTH DAY YEAR   AREA CODE

DELIBERATELY FURNISHING (OR CAUSING TO BE FURNISHED) FALSE INFORMATION ON THIS APPLICATION IS A CRIME PUNISHABLE BY FINE OR IMPRISONMENT, OR BOTH.

16 YOUR SIGNATURE

▶ _____

17 YOUR RELATIONSHIP TO THE PERSON IN ITEM 1 IS:

☐ Self ☐ Natural Or Adoptive Parent ☐ Legal Guardian ☐ Other (Specify)

Form **SS-5** (5/88)   1/85, 8/85, and 11/86 editions may be used until supply is exhausted

ON-THE-JOB SKILLS: ALPHABETIZING INFORMATION

Businesses handle a large amount of data, or information. Even though much of the data is kept on computers, some of it is also kept in file cabinets. Information in a file cabinet must be organized so that it can be found quickly. This is why the drawers of a file cabinet are usually arranged in **alphabetical order.** Things in alphabetical order are arranged according to the letters of the alphabet—A before B, B before C, and C before D, etc.

The exercises on the following pages explain the basic rules for filing documents in alphabetical order.

FILING RULES

1. **Things are usually filed according to a last name.** The person's last name is written first, followed by a comma and the person's first name.

Study the following examples:

Meribel Elena Soto *becomes* Soto, Meribel Elena

Robert A. Miller *becomes* Miller, Robert A.

❖ Exercise One

Directions:

Write each name in Column 1 with the last name first in Column 2.

Column 1	Column 2
Hector Allen Ortiz	_____
Betty A. Simpson	_____
Carl David Richards	_____

2. The last name closest to the beginning of the alphabet comes first.

Study the following examples:

Allen, Edward

Gonzalez, Sam

Parker, Gloria

Sosa, Pedro

A *before* G

G *before* P

P *before* S

❖ *Exercise Two*

Directions:

Write each name in Column 1 in alphabetical order in Column 2.

Column 1	Column 2
Sanchez, Ana Marie	_____
Donaldson, Howard R.	_____
Perry, Marilyn Marie	_____
Mendez, Henry Alfredo	_____

3. If the last name of two or more persons is the same, the first name closest to the beginning of the alphabet comes first.

Study the following examples:

Clark, Allen

Clark, Gloria

Clark, John

Garcia, Carlos

Garcia, Dora

❖ Exercise Three

Directions:

Write each name in Column 1 in alphabetical order in Column 2.

Column 1	Column 2
Hayes, William	_____
Martinez, Evelyn	_____
Hayes, Carolyn	_____
Martinez, José	_____
Hayes, Michael	_____

---

4. If the first and last names are exactly the same, the middle name or middle initial closest to the beginning of the alphabet comes first.

Study the following examples.

Brown, Alice **D.**	Cruz, Alfredo
Brown, Alice Mary	Cruz, Alfredo **L.**
	Cruz, Alfredo **R**oberto

❖ Exercise Four

Directions:

Write each name in Column 1 in alphabetical order in Column 2.

Column 1	Column 2
Diaz, Diana Rosa	_____
Bell, John M.	_____
Diaz, Diana B.	_____
Bell, John	_____
Bell, John Louis	_____

5. **When the last names begin with the same letters, the first different letter which is closest to the beginning of the alphabet comes first.** Or in a case like *Lee* and *Leed*, *Lee* comes first before *Leed*, since *Leed* has an extra letter. Study the following examples:

Lee, Nancy	Bac**on**, Janet
Lee**d**, Joseph	Bac**ow**, Robert B.
Lee**ds**, Jack B.	Ba**ter**, Bill
Lee**dson**, Jane	Ba**tes**, Nancy

❖ *Exercise Five*

Directions:

Write each name from Column 1 in alphabetical order in Column 2.

Column 1	Column 2
Thompson, Cindy	_____
Thombs, Martin	_____
Thomas, Lester	_____
Thomason, Susan	_____
Thomson, Fred	_____

6. **Let's say two last names are the same. One has a first initial and the other a first name with the same initial. <u>Write the first initial</u> before the first name.** Study the following examples:

Larson, **A.**	Perez, **C.**
Larson, **Allen**	Perez, **Carmen**
Lawson, Arnold	
Lawson, Carl	

7. **If the last name and the first name are the same, the name with a middle name or initial closest to the beginning of the alphabet is listed first.** Study the examples:

Johnson, Barbara

Johnson, Barbara Elaine

Johnson, Barbara Ann

Johnson, Barbara Marie

Johnson, Barbara E.

❖ *Exercise Six*

Directions:

Write each name from Column 1 in alphabetical order in Column 2.

Column 1	Column 2
Reamer, John	_____
Ream, A.	_____
Reamer, John A.	_____
Ream, Anna B.	_____
Reamer, J.	_____
Ream, John D.	_____
Ream, Arthur	_____

8. **The prefixes *Mac* and *Mc* are filed exactly as they are spelled.** Study the following examples:

Mabee, James

Mason, Paulette

MacArthur

McArthur, Joann

Macauley, Ronald

McBride, George

MacDonald, Robert

McGee, Alice

MacFarland, Horace

McNeil, Robert

❖ Exercise Seven

Directions:

List the following names from Column 1 in alphabetical order in Column 2.

Column 1	Column 2
MacDuff, Edward	_____
MacDermid, Thomas	_____
McDonald, Ray	_____
MacBride, Sally	_____
Marby, Shirley	_____
Macon, Sam	_____
McMullen, Rita	_____
MacGregor, John	_____
Mazza, Ben	_____
McCarthy, Diane	_____

❖ Exercise Eight

Directions:

Assume you are a file clerk in an office. The drawers in the cabinet pictured at the top of the following page hold records of your company's clients. You want to locate the records of the clients listed below the picture. After each name, write the number of the drawer in which that record should be kept. Study the examples.

1 Aa-As	**5** Cf-Cm	**9** Fa-Fz	**13** La-Lz	**17** Pa-Pr	**21** Sl-Sz
2 At-Bd	**6** Cn-Cz	**10** G-H	**14** Ma-Mn	**18** Ps-Q	**22** Ta-Tz
3 Be-Bz	**7** Da-Dz	**11** I-J	**15** Mo-Mz	**19** Ra-Rz	**23** U-V-W
4 Ca-Ce	**8** Ea-Ez	**12** Ka-Kz	**16** N-O	**20** Sa-Sk	**24** X-Y-Z

Example 1. Richard P. Lane __13__

Example 2. Steven Quinton __18__

1. Sarah L. Miles _____
2. Melvin W. Bard _____
3. Samuel C. Mann _____
4. Nancy Diaz _____
5. T.M. Carson _____
6. Adam Navarro _____
7. Francis Lee _____
8. Shirley Cheng _____
9. Arthur Kass _____
10. Lee Martin _____
11. Frank Goode _____
12. Ann M. White _____

13. Joyce Wilson _____
14. Jeanette Prevo _____
15. Edgar Collins _____
16. Frank Reno _____
17. James Taylor _____
18. Nancy Wong _____
19. Dennis Delavy _____
20. Steven Dadich _____
21. Tom Villeunova _____
22. Tom Breloski _____
23. Mary Deursin _____
24. David Toth _____
25. Ann LaRosa _____

❖ Exercise Nine

Directions:

Assume you are an assistant in the library. Put the following magazines back on the rack. Arrange the magazines in Column 1 in alphabetical order. Write their names in order on the lines in Column 2. The first one is done for you.

<table>
<tr><td align="center">**Column 1**</td><td colspan="2" align="center">**Column 2**</td></tr>
<tr><td>Vogue</td><td>1.</td><td>*American Artist*</td></tr>
<tr><td>Esquire</td><td>2.</td><td></td></tr>
<tr><td>Travel Magazine</td><td>3.</td><td></td></tr>
<tr><td>House Beautiful</td><td>4.</td><td></td></tr>
<tr><td>American Home</td><td>5.</td><td></td></tr>
<tr><td>Today's Secretary</td><td>6.</td><td></td></tr>
<tr><td>American Artist</td><td>7.</td><td></td></tr>
<tr><td>Business Week</td><td>8.</td><td></td></tr>
<tr><td>House and Garden</td><td>9.</td><td></td></tr>
<tr><td>Outdoor Life</td><td>10.</td><td></td></tr>
</table>

❖ Exercise Ten

Directions:

Again, arrange the following magazines in alphabetical order.

<table>
<tr><td>Current History</td><td>1.</td><td></td></tr>
<tr><td>Gourmet</td><td>2.</td><td></td></tr>
<tr><td>Trailer Life</td><td>3.</td><td></td></tr>
<tr><td>Money</td><td>4.</td><td></td></tr>
<tr><td>Skiing Magazine</td><td>5.</td><td></td></tr>
<tr><td>Apartment Life</td><td>6.</td><td></td></tr>
<tr><td>Popular Photography</td><td>7.</td><td></td></tr>
<tr><td>Interior Design</td><td>8.</td><td></td></tr>
<tr><td>Popular Mechanics</td><td>9.</td><td></td></tr>
<tr><td>Coin World</td><td>10.</td><td></td></tr>
</table>

❖ Exercise Eleven

Directions:

Read over the list of states on the left side. Arrange them in alphabetical order. Write their names in alphabetical order beginning with *Alabama* on Line 1 and ending with *Wyoming* on Line 50.

Nebraska	South Carolina	1. _____	26. _____
Florida	California	2. _____	27. _____
Oregon	Mississippi	3. _____	28. _____
New York	Alabama	4. _____	29. _____
Illinois	North Dakota	5. _____	30. _____
Arizona	Georgia	6. _____	31. _____
Ohio	North Carolina	7. _____	32. _____
Virginia	Oklahoma	8. _____	33. _____
Kentucky	New Jersey	9. _____	34. _____
Maryland	Pennsylvania	10. _____	35. _____
Washington	Colorado	11. _____	36. _____
New Mexico	Rhode Island	12. _____	37. _____
Texas	New Hampshire	13. _____	38. _____
Alaska	West Virginia	14. _____	39. _____
Hawaii	Delaware	15. _____	40. _____
Indiana	Utah	16. _____	41. _____
Maine	Tennessee	17. _____	42. _____
Vermont	Massachusetts	18. _____	43. _____
Michigan	South Dakota	19. _____	44. _____
Iowa	Montana	20. _____	45. _____
Nevada	Louisiana	21. _____	46. _____
Kansas	Arkansas	22. _____	47. _____
Missouri	Connecticut	23. _____	48. _____
Idaho	Minnesota	24. _____	49. _____
Wisconsin	Wyoming	25. _____	50. _____

❖ Exercise Twelve

Directions:

Assume you are a clerk in an office. Arrange the following customers' records in alphabetical order so that they will be easy to locate. Write the last names first, and use commas to separate last names from first names. The first listing has been done for you.

Column 1	Column 2
Michael A. Johnson	1. _Anderson, Susan J._
Betty C. Peterson	2. _____
Robert K. Clark	3. _____
Thomas B. Ross	4. _____
Victor L. Mendez	5. _____
Kathlene M. Carson	6. _____
Susan J. Anderson	7. _____
Arnold S. Clarkson	8. _____
Beth Ann Miller	9. _____
Rita E. Peters	10. _____
Constance R. Rossi	11. _____
Ronald F. Salvini	12. _____
John Vasquez	13. _____
Marilyn R. Taylor	14. _____
Allen R. Stevik	15. _____
Elizabeth A. Carr	16. _____
Ellen Rossman	17. _____
Anna O'Connor	18. _____
Barbara McBride	19. _____
Mary Ann MacDonald	20. _____

❖ Exercise Thirteen

Directions:

Assume you are a library assistant. Books by the authors in Column 1 have been returned to you. Put them in order according to each author's last name.

Write each last name first, followed by a comma and the first name. *James Baldwin* comes first. Write his name after 1. as *Baldwin, James.*

Column 1	Column 2
James A. Michener	1. _____
Leon Uris	2. _____
Mark Twain	3. _____
Jack London	4. _____
Edgar Allen Poe	5. _____
Richard Wright	6. _____
James Baldwin	7. _____
George Orwell	8. _____
Sinclair Lewis	9. _____
Joseph Conrad	10. _____
Margaret Mitchell	11. _____
John Steinbeck	12. _____
Herman Melville	13. _____
Arthur Hailey	14. _____
Henry Fielding	15. _____
Herman Wouk	16. _____
Ernest Hemingway	17. _____
Lawrence Durrell	18. _____
Kathleen Winsor	19. _____
Ian Fleming	20. _____

❖❖❖

ON-THE-JOB SKILLS: TELEPHONE MESSAGES

Employees in a company are not always at their desks to receive telephone calls. This is why the person answering the phone must be prepared to take down telephone messages for other employees.

The person writing the message may have telephone message slips like the ones below. This type of form makes it easy to include all the information quickly and accurately.

A telephone message slip must be filled out neatly with accurate spelling. Let's look at the telephone message slip that Maxine Patterson filled out for Mr. Richard Valez.

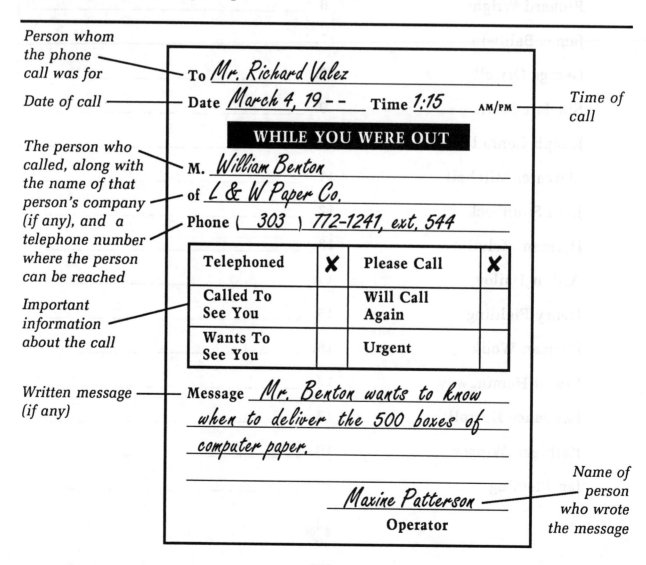

Person whom the phone call was for

To *Mr. Richard Valez*

Date of call

Date *March 4, 19 - -* Time *1:15* AM/PM

Time of call

WHILE YOU WERE OUT

The person who called, along with the name of that person's company (if any), and a telephone number where the person can be reached

M. *William Benton*
of *L & W Paper Co.*
Phone (*303*) *772-1241, ext. 544*

Important information about the call

Telephoned	✗	Please Call	✗
Called To See You		Will Call Again	
Wants To See You		Urgent	

Written message (if any)

Message *Mr. Benton wants to know when to deliver the 500 boxes of computer paper.*

Maxine Patterson
Operator

Name of person who wrote the message

❖ Exercise One

A few minutes later Maxine took a second call.

Directions:

As you read over the telephone conversation, help Maxine fill out the telephone message slip at the right.

Note: The time is now 1:20 PM on March 4.

—— *(The telephone rings)* ——

Maxine: Good Afternoon, Clark Office Supply Company.

Mr. Ross: May I speak to Mr. Anderson?

Maxine: I'll ring his office. (pause) He is not in. Can I take a message?

Mr. Ross: Yes, ask him to call me back as soon as possible.

Maxine: May I have your name?

Mr. Ross: Sure, this is Mr. Ross from Atco Business Machines.

Maxine: And may I have your telephone number?

Mr. Ross: 241-1000, extension 301.

Maxine: Is there a message you would like to leave for Mr. Anderson?

Mr. Ross: Yes, tell him that I have two new fax machines to show him.

Maxine: I will give Mr. Anderson your message as soon as he returns.

Mr. Ross: Thank you very much. Goodbye.

Maxine: You're welcome. Goodbye.

—— *(Both persons hang up.)* ——

To _____
Date _____ Time _____ AM/PM
WHILE YOU WERE OUT
M. _____
of _____
Phone (_____)_____

Telephoned		Please Call	
Called To See You		Will Call Again	
Wants To See You		Urgent	

Message _____
_____
_____
_____

_____
Operator

❖ Exercise Two

When Maxine writes a message on a telephone message slip, she changes some of the exact words which the caller uses. For example, Mr. Ross wants Maxine to tell Mr. Anderson, "*I* have two new adding machines to show *him*." She had to change the pronouns in the telephone message. She wrote the message as "*He* has two new adding machines to show *you*."

Maxine took another call, for Miss Lynn from Mr. Falk. Mr. Falk said, "*I* want *Miss Lynn* to call me as soon as possible." She wrote the message as "*He* wants *you* to call *him* as soon as possible."

Directions:

Rewrite the following messages for Maxine:

1. Mr. Stewart wants Maxine to tell Mr. Sanchez:

   "*I* need 16 boxes of file folders."

   _____

2. Mrs. Payne wants Maxine to tell Miss Richards:

   "*I* want to show *her* the new design for the desk calendars."

   _____

   _____

3. Mr. Russo wants Maxine to tell Mr. Arnold:

   "*I* am not satisfied with the new computers you loaned *me*. Can *I* have another one?"

   _____

   _____

   _____

❖ Exercise Three

Directions:

You are relieving Maxine while she is at lunch. Use the telephone message slips on the next page to write messages for each call below. Sign your name for "Operator." Note that the date for all of these calls is March 4.

1. A call came in for Wayne Cook at 1:40 p.m. from Miss Lucy Smith of the Mitchell Printing Company.

   A. Her telephone number is 963-1240.

   B. She will call again.

   C. Message: She needs more information on the order from March 1.

2. A call came in for Mrs. Elaine Carter at 1:45 p.m. from Mark Ivory of the Ivory Law Firm.

   A. His telephone number is 772-1423.

   B. He wants Mrs. Carter to call him as soon as she gets back.

   C. Message: He needs more information about the contracts.

3. A call came in for Mr. Frank Garcia at 1:45 p.m. from Ralph Thomas of the Lewis Insurance Agency.

   A. Mr. Thomas' telephone number is 468-1233, Extension 800.

   B. He wants Mr. Garcia to call him.

   C. Message: He will not be able to meet him for lunch tomorrow at 12:30 p.m.

4. A call came in for Mr. Chou at 2:00 p.m., from Mrs. Ann Finch of the Bond Construction Company.

   A. Her telephone number is 772-2148, Extension 606.

   B. She called to see him.

   C. Message: She would like to pick up 2 boxes of typing paper and 1 box of pens at 3:00 p.m.

(1)

To _____

Date _____ Time _____ AM/PM

WHILE YOU WERE OUT

M. _____

of _____

Phone (_____)_____

Telephoned		Please Call	
Called To See You		Will Call Again	
Wants To See You		Urgent	

Message _____

_____

_____

_____

_____
Operator

(2)

To _____

Date _____ Time _____ AM/PM

WHILE YOU WERE OUT

M. _____

of _____

Phone (_____)_____

Telephoned		Please Call	
Called To See You		Will Call Again	
Wants To See You		Urgent	

Message _____

_____

_____

_____

_____
Operator

(3)

To _____

Date _____ Time _____ AM/PM

WHILE YOU WERE OUT

M. _____

of _____

Phone (_____)_____

Telephoned		Please Call	
Called To See You		Will Call Again	
Wants To See You		Urgent	

Message _____

_____

_____

_____

_____
Operator

(4)

To _____

Date _____ Time _____ AM/PM

WHILE YOU WERE OUT

M. _____

of _____

Phone (_____)_____

Telephoned		Please Call	
Called To See You		Will Call Again	
Wants To See You		Urgent	

Message _____

_____

_____

_____

_____
Operator

❖ Exercise Four

Directions:

Assume you are a receptionist at the Diamond Baking Company. Use the telephone message slips on the next page to write messages for each of the following calls. Sign your name for "Operator." Assume today's date is December 14 (you can write it down as 12/14).

1. Ned Finklestein received a telephone call at 11:08 a.m. from Sam Miller of the Hill-Seven Market.

   A. Mr. Miller's telephone number is 542-1518.

   B. He wants to see Mr. Finklestein.

   C. Message: He needs 12 loaves of white bread, 6 loaves of whole wheat bread, 4 loaves of butter bread, and 6 packages of hot dog rolls.

2. A call came in for Maria Rodriguez at 11:15 a.m. from Louis Ball of Big Lou's Market.

   A. His telephone number is 341-2121.

   B. He wants Mrs. Rodriguez to call him.

   C. It is urgent.

   D. Message: He needs more bread and rolls. He did not receive a complete order yesterday.

3. Bud Carson received a telephone call at 11:20 a.m. from Mr. Mike Hargrave of the Miller Food Store.

   A. Mr. Hargrave's telephone number is 824-9100.

   B. It is urgent.

   C. Message: He needs his order by 2:00 p.m. instead of 4:00 p.m.

4. A call came in for Nancy Allen at 11:24 a.m. from Gordon Sapio of the Royale Castle Cafeteria.

   A. Mr. Sapio's telephone number is 293-1420.

   B. He wants Nancy Allen to call him.

   C. He needs 10 loaves of bread, 8 packages of hamburger rolls, and 6 packages of hot dog rolls.

(1)

To _____

Date _____ Time _____ AM/PM

WHILE YOU WERE OUT

M. _____

of _____

Phone (_____)_____

Telephoned		Please Call	
Called To See You		Will Call Again	
Wants To See You		Urgent	

Message _____

_____

_____

_____

_____

Operator

(2)

To _____

Date _____ Time _____ AM/PM

WHILE YOU WERE OUT

M. _____

of _____

Phone (_____)_____

Telephoned		Please Call	
Called To See You		Will Call Again	
Wants To See You		Urgent	

Message _____

_____

_____

_____

_____

Operator

(3)

To _____

Date _____ Time _____ AM/PM

WHILE YOU WERE OUT

M. _____

of _____

Phone (_____)_____

Telephoned		Please Call	
Called To See You		Will Call Again	
Wants To See You		Urgent	

Message _____

_____

_____

_____

_____

Operator

(4)

To _____

Date _____ Time _____ AM/PM

WHILE YOU WERE OUT

M. _____

of _____

Phone (_____)_____

Telephoned		Please Call	
Called To See You		Will Call Again	
Wants To See You		Urgent	

Message _____

_____

_____

_____

_____

Operator

❖ Exercise Five

You don't always have a telphone answer pad in front of you when you answer a call. But you should still be prepared to take down each telephone message completely and accurately.

Directions:

Assume you are assigned to answer the telephone in the Customer Service Department of the Citizen's National Bank. Write up each of the following messages in the blank spaces provided. Assume today's date is Sept. 29. Be sure to sign your name at the bottom of each message.

The first message has been written out for you.

1. Bill Conti, the Office Manager, received a telephone call at 12:06 p.m. from Miss Ortiz in the Personnel Department.

   A. Her extension number is 146.

   B. Please call her.

   C. Message: She has a job applicant for him to interview tomorrow at 10:00 a.m.

   Bill Conti   Sept. 29, 12:06 p.m.

   Miss Ortiz of Personnel called. Her ext. 146. Please call.

   She has job applicant for you to interview tomorrow at 10:00 a.m.

   (your signature)

2. A call came in for Joan O'Brien at 12:09 p.m. from Miss Atler of the Loan Department.

   A. She wants Miss O'Brien to call her back.

   B. Her extension is 298.

   C. It is urgent.

   D. Message: There will be a special meeting tomorrow in her office at 9:00 a.m. Call for details.

3. A call came in for Barbara Cobb at 12:13 p.m. from Ms. Edwards of the Accounts Receivable Department of the First National Bank.

   A. Ms. Edwards' telephone number is 863-2244, Ext. 103.

   B. She wants Miss Cobb to call her back.

   C. It is important.

   D. Message: She has eight bad checks from the Citizen's National Bank that she is returning.

   _____

   _____

   _____

   _____

4. A call came in for Donald Sawyer at 12:20 p.m. from Thomas Blake of the Mortgage Department.

   A. His extension is 489.

   B. He will call again.

   C. Message: He wants to discuss Mr. Williams' checking account.

   _____

   _____

   _____

   _____

ON-THE-JOB SKILLS: SCHEDULING APPOINTMENTS

Many types of employees in today's business world are required to schedule appointments for other employees.

For example:

- A secretary in an office.
- A nurse in a doctor's office.
- A receptionist.

Many other types of employees are required to keep good records for themselves of their daily appointments.

For example:

- Sales representatives.
- Service representatives going out on appointments.
- People in auto repair garages.
- Counselors.

You should become familiar with appointment books and the procedure for filling them out. It is a simple procedure. Let's look at an example.

MAKING A DENTAL APPOINTMENT

Hector Santos works as a secretary in a dentist's office. He makes appointments for patients. For each appointment, he checks the appointment book to find out the day and the time the dentist or dental hygienist is free.

—— *(Telephone rings.)* ——

Hector: Good afternoon, Dr. Chou's office.

Mrs. Moran: This is Mrs. Moran calling. I just received my reminder to come in for my six-month dental check-up, and I would like to make an appointment.

Hector: The dental hygienist comes in on Tuesdays, Fridays, and Saturdays. Let me check the appointment book to find out when she can see you. Can you hold the line while I check the appointment book?

Mrs. Moran: Yes.

(He presses the hold button on the telephone. He looks in the appointment book and thumbs through the pages. He then presses the extension which Mrs. Moran is on.)

Hector: Hello, Mrs. Moran? Thank you for waiting.

Mrs. Moran: You're welcome.

Hector: The dental hygienist can see you on Friday, July 15, at 2:30 P.M. Is this date and time convenient for you?

Mrs. Moran: No, I'll be out of town on July 15. Do you have an appointment for the following week?

Hector: Just a minute. Let me check.

(Hector turns a few pages in the appointment book to the following week.)

Mrs. Moran, can you come in on Saturday, July 23, at 10:00 A.M.?

Mrs. Moran: Yes, that will be fine.

Hector: I'll write your appointment in the appointment book. May I have your telephone number, Mrs. Moran?

Mrs. Moran: Sure. 972-3496.

Hector: If you cannot keep your appointment, please call me at least 24 hours in advance so that I can give the appointment to another patient.

Mrs. Moran: Okay. Thank you very much. Goodbye.

Hector: Goodbye.

—(Hector and Mrs. Moran hang up their telephone receivers.)—

Hector recorded Mrs. Moran's appointment in the appointment book for the dental hygienist. He records each appointment in pencil. Look at line 7 on the page from the dentist's appointment book on the next page.

(1)	APPOINTMENTS FOR SATURDAY, JULY 23, 19--		
(2)	Time (A)	Name of Patient (B)	Phone No. (C)
(3)	8:00 A.M.		
(4)	8:30 A.M.		
(5)	9:00 A.M.		
(6)	9:30 A.M.	Mr. Jack Martin	324-1496
(7)	10:00 A.M.	Mrs. Moran	972-3496
(8)	10:30 A.M.		
(9)	11:00 A.M.		
(10)	11:30 A.M.		
(11)	12:00 P.M.		
(12)	12:30 P.M.		
(13)	1:00 P.M.	Mr. Tom DeMateo	751-3486
(14)	1:30 P.M.	Ms. Rita Pérez	874-1894 work: 983-1818

The appointment book contains the following information:

1. The day and the date (See line 1).

2. The time of each appointment. (See Column A.)

   Most appointments are scheduled at one-half hour intervals.

3. The name of the patient in Column B.

4. The patient's telephone number in Column C.

The appointment times for 8:00 A.M. to 9:00 A.M. are crossed out because the first appointment is scheduled for 9:30 A.M. The appointment times for 12:00 P.M. and 12:30 P.M. are crossed out because this is lunchtime.

When a patient makes an appointment in person (as opposed to on the phone), Hector fills out a dental appointment card as shown on the next page.

The dental appointment card contains the following information:

1. The name of the patient. *(See line 1.)*

2. The day of the dental appointment. *(See line 2.)*

3. The date and time of the appointment. *(See line 3.)*

4. The name of the dentist. *(See line 4.)*

5. The address of the dentist's office. *(See line 5.)*

6. The phone number of the dentist's office. *(See line 6.)*

7. Information on *lines 7, 8, 9, and 10.* The patient is asked to give 24 hours' notice if the appointment cannot be kept. This way the appointment can be given to another patient. A patient who does not give notice of a cancellation may be charged for the appointment.

(1) **M** *rs. Jean Miller*

Has An Appointment On

(2) ___ Mon. **X** Tues. ___ Wed. ___ Thurs. ___ Fri. ___ Sat.

(3) Date *July 19, 19—* At *1:30* A.M. (P.M.)

(4) With Dr. Edward Chou D.D.S.

(5) 1389 Greenfield Road

(6) Phone: Office 389-1211

(7) Please give 24 hours' notice

(8) if you cannot keep this appointment.

(9) Other patients will appreciate your courtesy

(10) in releasing this time for them.

❖ Exercise One

Directions:

Help Hector schedule appointments for each person below.

1. Schedule an appointment for Kevan Edwards at 11:00 A.M. on Saturday, July 23.

A. Fill out the first dental appointment card on the next page.

B. Record the appointment on line 9 on page 121. Kevan's telephone number is 482-3488.

2. Schedule an appointment for Eva
   Rosada at 10:30 A.M. on Saturday,
   July 23.

   A. Fill out the second dental
      appointment card below.

   B. Record the appointment on line 8
      on page 121. Eva's telephone
      number is 325-2477.

M _____

Has An Appointment On

__ Mon. __ Tues. __ Wed. __ Thurs. __ Fri. __ Sat.

Date _____ At _____ A.M. P.M.

With Dr. Edward Chou D.D.S.
1389 Greenfield Road
Phone: Office 389-1211

Please give 24 hours' notice
if you cannot keep this appointment.
Other patients will appreciate your courtesy
in releasing this time for them.

M _____

Has An Appointment On

__ Mon. __ Tues. __ Wed. __ Thurs. __ Fri. __ Sat.

Date _____ At _____ A.M. P.M.

With Dr. Edward Chou D.D.S.
1389 Greenfield Road
Phone: Office 389-1211

Please give 24 hours' notice
if you cannot keep this appointment.
Other patients will appreciate your courtesy
in releasing this time for them.

❖ Exercise Two

Directions:

Help Hector schedule appointments for patients on September 14, 19__, on page 125 and September 15, 19__, on page 126. Record each appointment in the appointment book in pencil.

Make the following notations in the appointment book:

    A. For September 14, cross out the times for 12:30 P.M. and 1:00 P.M. and 5:30 to and including 9:00 P.M.

    B. For September 15, cross out the times for 8:00 A.M. and 8:30 A.M., 12:30 P.M. and 1:00 P.M., and 7:00 P.M. to and including 9:00 P.M.

1. Schedule an appointment for Marie Paul at 3:00 P.M. on Thursday, September 15.

    A. Fill out a dental appointment card on page 127. (The appointment is being made in the office.)

    B. Record the appointment on line 17 on page 126. Marie's telephone number is 388-1499.

2. Schedule an appointment for Juan Matos at 4:00 P.M. on Thursday, September 15. Record the appointment on page 126. Juan's telephone number is 924-3880.

3. Schedule an appointment for Peter Belini at 9:00 A.M. on Wednesday, September 14.

    A. Fill out a dental appointment card on page 127.

    B. Record the appointment on page 125. Peter's telephone number is 388-2411.

4. Rita Moore calls to schedule an appointment for 9:30 A.M. on Wednesday, September 14. Record the appointment in the appointment book. Rita's telephone number is 332-9822.

5. Peter Belini calls to change his appointment at 9:00 A.M. on Wednesday, September 14.

    A. Erase his appointment.

    B. Schedule a new appointment for 4:30 on Thursday, September 15. Include his telephone number.

	Time	Name of Patient	Phone No.
(1)		**APPOINTMENTS FOR WEDNESDAY, SEPTEMBER 14, 19--**	
(3)	8:00 A.M.		
(4)	8:30 A.M.		
(5)	9:00 A.M.		
(6)	9:30 A.M.		
(7)	10:00 A.M.		
(8)	10:30 A.M.		
(9)	11:00 A.M.		
(10)	11:30 A.M.	*Claire Hopper*	*972-3496*
(11)	12:00 P.M.		
(12)	12:30 P.M.		
(13)	1:00 P.M.		
(14)	1:30 P.M.		
(15)	2:00 P.M.	*Edwin Lawson*	*297-3912*
(16)	2:30 P.M.		
(17)	3:00 P.M.		
(18)	3:30 P.M.		
(19)	4:00 P.M.	*Linda Collins*	*329-1032 work: 874-0804*
(20)	4:30 P.M.		
(21)	5:00 P.M.		
(22)	5:30 P.M.		
(23)	6:00 P.M.		
(24)	6:30 P.M.		
(25)	7:00 P.M.		
(26)	7:30 P.M.		
(27)	8:00 P.M.		
(28)	8:30 P.M.		
(29)	9:00 P.M.		

	Time	Name of Patient	Phone No.
(1)	**APPOINTMENTS FOR THURSDAY, SEPTEMBER 15, 19--**		
(2)	Time	Name of Patient	Phone No.
(3)	8:00 A.M.		
(4)	8:30 A.M.		
(5)	9:00 A.M.		
(6)	9:30 A.M.		
(7)	10:00 A.M.		
(8)	10:30 A.M.	Diana Murphy	968-4191
(9)	11:00 A.M.	Luis Vargas	924-4238
(10)	11:30 A.M.		
(11)	12:00 P.M.		
(12)	12:30 P.M.		
(13)	1:00 P.M.		
(14)	1:30 P.M.	Melissa Daniels	332-9822
(15)	2:00 P.M.	Ricardo Diaz	462-1190
(16)	2:30 P.M.		
(17)	3:00 P.M.		
(18)	3:30 P.M.		
(19)	4:00 P.M.		
(20)	4:30 P.M.		
(21)	5:00 P.M.	Yvette Garcia	297-4868
(22)	5:30 P.M.	Maria Sanchez	332-9872
(23)	6:00 P.M.		
(24)	6:30 P.M.		
(25)	7:00 P.M.		
(26)	7:30 P.M.		
(27)	8:00 P.M.		
(28)	8:30 P.M.		
(29)	9:00 P.M.		

M _____

Has An Appointment On

__ Mon. __ Tues. __ Wed. __ Thurs. __ Fri. __ Sat.

Date _____ At _____ A.M.
P.M.

With Dr. Edward Chou D.D.S.

1389 Greenfield Road

Phone: Office 389-1211

Please give 24 hours' notice
if you cannot keep this appointment.
Other patients will appreciate your courtesy
in releasing this time for them.

M _____

Has An Appointment On

__ Mon. __ Tues. __ Wed. __ Thurs. __ Fri. __ Sat.

Date _____ At _____ A.M.
P.M.

With Dr. Edward Chou D.D.S.

1389 Greenfield Road

Phone: Office 389-1211

Please give 24 hours' notice
if you cannot keep this appointment.
Other patients will appreciate your courtesy
in releasing this time for them.

STATE ABBREVIATIONS

Alabama	AL	Montana	MT
Alaska	AK	Nebraska	NE
Arizona	AZ	New Hampshire	NH
Arkansas	AR	New Jersey	NJ
California	CA	New Mexico	NM
Colorado	CO	New York	NY
Connecticut	CT	Nevada	NV
Delaware	DE	North Carolina	NC
Florida	FL	North Dakota	ND
Georgia	GA	Ohio	OH
Hawaii	HI	Oklahoma	OK
Idaho	ID	Oregon	OR
Illinois	IL	Pennsylvania	PA
Indiana	IN	Rhode Island	RI
Iowa	IA	South Carolina	SC
Kansas	KS	South Dakota	SD
Kentucky	KY	Tennessee	TN
Louisiana	LA	Texas	TX
Maine	ME	Utah	UT
Maryland	MD	Vermont	VT
Massachusetts	MA	Virginia	VA
Michigan	MI	Washington	WA
Minnesota	MN	West Virginia	WV
Mississippi	MS	Wisconsin	WI
Missouri	MO	Wyoming	WY